Praise for *Your Goal Guide*

"Everyone says they have goals. But far, far fewer actually take the time to set out a plan to achieve them. With *Your Goal Guide*, Debra Eckerling has given you the roadmap to do just that."

—Peter Shankman, author of *Faster Than Normal: Turbocharge Your Focus, Productivity, and Success with the Secrets of the ADHD Brain*

"Debra is clearly rooting for your success through this inspiring book! Her authenticity and honest intentions are so visible in each chapter. *Your Goal Guide* is an excellent book for all those who are ready to bloom and rewrite their story."

—Chandresh Bhardwaj, a seventh generation spiritual advisor and author of *Break the Norms*

"Thank you, Debra Eckerling, for literally providing us with a roadmap to achieve our goals. Whether you are a stay-at-home mom or dad, a college student, a corporate employee, or an entrepreneur, you will benefit from *Your Goal Guide*, which clearly outlines the steps you need to live the vibrant life that you want. Perhaps the most poignant part of Debra Eckerling's book is the realization that most of us spend more time deciding on and planning where we want to go on vacation than how we want to live our lives. Without a clear vision, we wander aimlessly—wondering why we are not happy or fulfilled. By using *Your Goal Guide*, we will have no more excuses for not getting to our desired destination. Thank you, Debra Eckerling! I can't wait to start my journey!"

—Elaine Hall, award-winning author, speaker, and founder of The Miracle Project profiled in the HBO documentary *Autism: The Musical*

"Debra Eckerling is the real deal. For years she has been one of the best guides I know for hundreds of writers. Writing a book and finding a home for that book can often feel like an impenetrable thicket, but Debra's The D*E*B Method is simple and wise. And *Your Goal Guide*, like Debra herself, is lovely and inspiring."

—**Amy Friedman, writing teacher and author, most recently of *Desperado's Wife***

"*Your Goal Guide* by Debra Eckerling is a must-read for anyone who has a goal and a desire to reach a destination. After deciding what you want, how do you get there? Debra guides you through actions you can take and valuable tools and techniques that will help you to reach anywhere your mind can travel. She draws from her experience. She is a guide who you will want to follow. If you see it and believe it, it can happen."

—**Jen Grisanti, story/career consultant, writing instructor for NBC, author, and speaker**

"One of things that is so helpful about *Your Goal Guide* is that it gives a detailed account for anyone who is trying to achieve their goals and gives a fresh perspective on how to get started. I know so many people who have a lot of trouble setting goals and affirmations, and this book will definitely guide them to where they need to be. I, for one, will definitely use this as a blueprint and so should others."

—**Jerod Williams, group exercise and fitness instructor**

"Debra Eckerling is the queen of helping people set and achieve their goals. It's like a sixth sense for her! And it really shines through in this guide that is a roadmap to success."

—**Madalyn Sklar, host of *#TwitterSmarter* podcast and chat**

"Deb Eckerling's *Your Goal Guide* is a thoughtful roadmap to help you get from here (the good idea) to there (actually accomplishing what you want to do). Worth reading. But don't just read it. Follow her instructions."

—Dr. Chaz Austin, EdD, president of Austin Career Packaging & Marketing

"It's a big, wide world of wonderful things out there, and deciding what you want is always the hardest part. Most goal setting guides assume that you already have a clear picture of what you want to achieve, which renders them useless (and frustrating). *Your Goal Guide* helps you set your vision for the future first, before diving into the steps on how to reach it. With specific exercises to help you narrow down the overwhelm and home in on what you want, this book is like a trusted friend or caring coach who asks the tough questions that lead you to where you need to go, and then gives you the gentle push you need to get there."

—Jennifer Ballard, marketing manager, *Social Media Examiner*

"What a refreshing read! Every guru tells us to set and achieve goals. But what if you need help figuring out exactly what you want in the first place, let alone how to get there? Debra Eckerling's very practical book helps us to do just that. It's like having a dear friend walk with you each step of the way, holding your hand, guiding you along your very own yellow brick road to the life of your dreams. Two thumbs way up!"

—Mari Smith, premier Facebook marketing expert and author of *The New Relationship Marketing*

"I just finished reading Deb Eckerling's *Your Goal Guide*, and it is making me wish she wrote this about fifteen years ago when...I was struggling (intensely) to write my doctoral dissertation and my first book. *Your Goal Guide* is a dream come true for someone who needs some structure and context when looking to make big changes. Not only is it jam-packed with life hacks that will expand your productivity and focus, it is laid out in a truly easy to follow manner, and written in a voice that is warm, and completely accessible. If you have ever struggled with achieving goals or navigating big changes, this book is for you."

—Dr. Michael Lennox, author of *Dream Sight, Llewellyn's Complete Dictionary of Dreams,* and *Llewellyn's Little Book of Dreams*

"Debra Eckerling makes so much sense that even a befuddled procrastinator like me is impressed. Her step-by-step approach is super easy to follow and moves past 'happy talk' to give you the tools you need to get your life moving in the right direction."

—Dennis Wilen, web producer, Pocho.com

"Every person sets goals at some point in their life but usually self-sabotages their efforts. Deb's book truly keeps you focused on your goals, allowing you to cancel out the noise that surrounds you, giving you concrete tips on how to achieve your dreams with a well-plotted path to success. Deb's a genuine inspiration!"

—Jeanne Veillette Bowerman, editor-in-chief of *Script Magazine,* senior editor of *Writer's Digest,* and cofounder and moderator of #Scriptchat

"*Your Goal Guide* could become the most complete book on goal-setting. Eckerling gets right down to the nitty-gritty instead of waving a wand of general advice and expecting a newbie to magically absorb the details."

—Carolyn Howard-Johnson, multi-award-winning author of *The Frugal Book Promoter* and *The Frugal Editor*

"So often, goal-setting is met with anxiety, overwhelm, and absolute confusion as to where to start even defining what our goals should be. Debra takes us through each step, making the reader feel accomplished along the way, and the end result is a crystal-clear roadmap as to what they're about to achieve. Brilliant!"

—Jessica Kupferman, cofounder of She Podcasts

"Debra Eckerling's *Your Goal Guide* will help many people finally reach their goals. Readers who follow the vision, especially those who feel stuck, will finally get their work done. As a client, I have firsthand experience of Debra's magic and continue to be a fan."

—Jeff Pulver, internet pioneer, VoIP; cofounder of Vonage

"You know the old saw, 'if you don't know where you're going, any road will get you there.' As appealing as that may sound, it also means you won't get anywhere close to reaching your goals if you don't chart your own path! Deb Eckerling's *Your Goal Guide* helps you build your own roadmap to the future, by breaking down the steps to success in an easy-to-digest manner. Gas up and get ready for the ride to Goaltopia!"

—Scott Perry, marketing consultant at Sperry Media

"Feeling a little unclear about your direction? Not quite sure how to move forward with a goal or intention? Never fear! Debra Eckerling's new book *Your Goal Guide: A Roadmap for Setting, Planning and Achieving Your Goals* is an incredibly helpful tool that will masterfully direct you toward achieving your goals and intentions in a clear, concise, and well thought out manner. No stone is left unturned as Debra helps you cover all of your bases and gets your plan and foundation rock solid! Not only will you move your goals and dreams in a forward motion, Debra's book will help you gain personal clarity and self-awareness which leads to confidence. A win-win all around!"

—G. Brian Benson, actor, speaker, and award-winning author of *Habits for Success: Inspired Ideas to Help You Soar*

"Finally, the roadmap we need for goal setting! Debra Eckerling is the master of goal setting, and in this book she shows us how each of us can successfully achieve goals with a clear plan. Being a perfectionist at heart, goal setting is the foundation for everything I do, and that's the reason why I loved this book. By using her signature The D*E*B Method, Debra teaches us how to Determine, Explore, and Brainstorm to accomplish our plan. Whether we're setting personal or professional goals, Debra has us covered!

"The book has a lovely flow, it's very easy to follow the step-by-step process, and I loved the analogy between goal setting and a road trip. After all, life is a journey, and we travel every day through each moment and experience, don't we?

"Get ready to be pleasantly surprised by your accomplishments with *Your Goal Guide!*"

—Sabrina Cadini, Holistic Life Coach

"Goal-setting! Task-management! Actionable to-do lists! Debra Eckerling gave me just what I needed. I can't wait to share her wisdom with my screenwriting clients and writing students."

—Pilar Alessandra, screenwriting instructor at On the Page and author of *The Coffee Break Screenwriter*

"If you ever dared to dream big, and then got stuck making it happen, Debra Eckerling's *Your Goal Guide* is your solution! The author takes you on a road trip to success using an easy-to-follow goal-setting process, roll-out plan and maintenance phase approach to keep things moving forward. Stop procrastinating, and take charge of your life dream today by reading and applying the tips in this must-have book!"

—Liz H Kelly, Goody PR founder and author of *8-Second PR*

"Wow! I loved *Your Goal Guide* by Debra Eckerling. I've always been into goal setting, but I think I've been missing a few key steps all this time! I agree...figuring out what it is you actually want is critical. It needs to start with some deep inner reflection and essentially, come from the soul.

"The D*E*B Method that she lays out is genius. I think 'Determining My Mission' has been fairly easy for me. But I have been challenged in the 'Exploring My Options' and 'Brainstorming My Path' parts. Thanks Debra, you have changed the way I think about my goals! Highly recommended."

—Jon Wuebben, CEO of Content Launch and author of *Future Marketing: Winning in the Prosumer Age*

"Your Goal Guide: A Roadmap for Setting, Planning and Achieving Your Goals could not have come at a better time. I am acutely aware that another shift in my life is looming on the horizon (that shift called retirement) and, unlike my work life, I have not yet any goals about what that is supposed to look like! (I mean—retirement is about not working, right?) Wrong! Goals are important to set at every stage of our lives! And what I love about Deb's book is that she helps us figure out what our true goals really are—not sales quotas we must meet or some kind of ambiguous 'I want to do **** someday.' But real, achievable and maybe BHA Goals!

"Her clarion call is to '...figure out how to set and reach your goals, while the rest of the world—and the rest of your life—is business as usual,' in such a way that you see a clear path to your new future and the steps you must make. I'm very much looking forward to moving forward in my journey with The D*E*B Method—from determining what I really want to do when I grow up (and retire), to unveiling the different options available before moving from my current position (or if I even want/need to), to creating a clear and achievable path, to finally achieving the new goals I set. Thanks, Deb, for writing the perfect book at the perfect time!"

—Viveka von Rosen, Chief Visibility Officer and cofounder at Vengreso

YOUR GOAL GUIDE

YOUR GOAL GUIDE

A ROADMAP FOR SETTING, PLANNING AND ACHIEVING YOUR GOALS

DEBRA ECKERLING

Mango Publishing

Published by Mango Publishing Group, a division of Mango Media Inc.

Cover Design: Jayoung Hong
Cover illustration: Jayoung Hong
Layout & Design: Jayoung Hong
Author Photo: Dave Johnson

For permission requests, please contact the publisher at:
Mango Publishing Group
2850 S Douglas Road, 2nd Floor
Coral Gables, FL 33134 USA
info@mango.bz

For special orders, quantity sales, course adoptions and corporate sales, please email the publisher at sales@mango.bz. For trade and wholesale sales, please contact Ingram Publisher Services at customer.service@ingramcontent.com or +1.800.509.4887.

Your Goal Guide: A Roadmap for Setting, Planning and Achieving Your Goals

Library of Congress Cataloging-in-Publication number: 2019948629
ISBN: (print) 978-1-64250-150-6, (ebook) 978-1-64250-151-3
BISAC category code: SEL035000—SELF-HELP / Self-Management / Time Management

Printed in the United States of America

For my mom, Arlene Leder.
You have always encouraged me to do what I love
and follow my heart. Thank you for all of your love,
inspiration, and support.

Table of Contents

INTRODUCTION
Navigating This Book

Before going on a road trip, you need the essentials: paper and pen, a map, and a destination. You want to make sure to have a full tank of gas, predetermined stopping points, and plenty of snacks. A plan gets you started. Fuel and motivation keep you going. The same is true for your goals. Your destination is GoalTopia: that ideal place where you achieve the objectives you set and live the life you want.

Hi, I'm Deb. And I love helping people set and achieve their goals.

My passion for goal-setting started several years ago, almost by accident. I was doing events for Barnes & Noble, and one of my customers asked if I'd start a writers' support group. I said, "If you think people will attend, I'd be happy to try it out."

It was a hit. And I saw the power of goal-setting and accountability firsthand.

At these meetings, people would share what they were working on, report on their goals, and set new ones. Almost everyone, including me, would get something done for the next meeting. Seeing others achieve is encouraging—"If they can do it, so can I"—but the positive feedback you get when you reach your goals is even more motivating. The process works!

Fast forward several years. I had moved to Los Angeles and frequently talked about this awesome goals group I led at Barnes & Noble. It was time to start it up again. Over the years, the group—which was named Write On!—has gone through many changes and now also embraces creatives and entrepreneurs. We have live meetings where I give out "stars"—a gold star when you achieve the goals you set, any color star for effort. There's also a substantial online community: a page and group on Facebook, as well as a #GoalChat on Twitter.

This group led me to start coaching after a member asked if I would help him one-on-one. I also began speaking and leading workshops, live and online. Over the years, I've helped people around the world set and achieve goals through strategizing, troubleshooting, and offering resources, encouragement, and deadlines. Their projects ranged from writing books and starting blogs to social media, business development, and more. I've also worked with businesses to turn their ideas into reality.

After years of working on and polishing my goal-setting and productivity techniques, I adapted it into a simple roadmap, The D*E*B Method, which is the process used in *Your Goal Guide*.

The Goal Conundrum

What stops you from achieving your goals?

- Not enough time?

- Not enough motivation?

- Not a clue as to what you want to do?

You're not alone.

It's difficult to focus on your goals when you have to invest time and energy you don't really have into something that *may* reward you down the line. However, if you make your goals a priority and work on them for short periods of time, you will eventually reach your desired destination.

The Roadmap

The D*E*B Method is the approach I created to help people figure out what they want and how to develop a plan to get it. The process, which we will go through in Part 1 of the book, is as simple as planning a road trip.

The first step—D—is to *Determine Where You Want to Go: Your Mission.* What type of place would you like to go on your road trip? What makes you happy? The beach, the mountains, the city? Do you want an adrenaline-fueled adventure, or would you rather relax at a resort?

Whether you are planning a trip or plotting a goal, you need to get a clear vision of where you want to go and what you want to accomplish. This section will help you figure out your GoalTopia and the mission behind it; this will serve as the driving force that propels you through your journey.

Once you know your ideal target, it's time to E—*Explore Different Destinations.* You know you want to go to an amusement park, but which one? You want to start a side business for fun and profit, but what type of business?

Just as there are more than four hundred amusement parks in the United States, there are countless options for side businesses. You need to narrow it down.

This section will guide you through investigating different possibilities. The legwork will help you find clarity, so you can choose a specific destination or goal.

After you set your sights on a long-term goal, there's B—*Brainstorm Your Route.* For a road trip, that means deciding when to drive, where to stop, and what sights to see along the way. For a project, you need to list out all the goals, benchmarks, and tasks. Gather the pieces, put together an itinerary, and create a clear path that leads to your goal.

Part 2 of the book, *Rules of the Road*, offers guidance including everything from *Tips for a Successful Trip*—time management and productivity—to *Car Maintenance and Troubleshooting*—staying on track and dealing with drama.

No matter your dreams, *Your Goal Guide* is the roadmap to help you set, plan, and achieve your goals.

Personal Versus Professional Goals

Although *Your Goal Guide* is geared toward professional aspirations, The D*E*B Method can be used for reaching personal goals as well. For instance, your mission might relate to having a healthier lifestyle or traveling more. You would then explore options and brainstorm a path to make it happen.

The other thing to keep in mind is that personal and professional goals work together. The things you do to improve your personal life may impact your professional life and vice versa. For instance, if you lead a healthier lifestyle, you will have more energy and be more productive at work. Or you may be out networking for work and make a new friend with similar interests. That could help you make progress on your personal goals.

My point: While one type of goal might be a priority over another in a certain phase of life, it's not ultimately a choice between one or the other. All goals work in tandem. They elevate each other and can give your travel a turbo-boost in the process.

Goal-Setting Simplified

The key word here is "simplified."

A lot of the time, people get stalled—or don't even get started—because they overcomplicate things. This book, like my process, is very user-friendly.

Your Goal Guide has:

- Simple exercises to get you thinking
- Sound advice that's short and to the point
- Troubleshooting tactics to deal with common problems
- Case studies that showcase examples
- Resources to keep you going

Beware of Backseat Drivers: Setting goals is a very personal process. You may be tempted to get advice from friends and loved ones while you are trying to figure things out. However, I recommend you keep any inquiries for feedback vague and limited to just one or two people until you come to your own conclusions. You don't want to be lured away from the right route or steered in the wrong direction.

You can also stop by the *Your Goal Guide* community on Facebook to ask questions at any time.

Goal-Setting Survey: I surveyed a variety of writers, creatives, consultants, marketers, and entrepreneurs to ask about their goal-setting habits and challenges. Some of their strategies and suggestions are incorporated throughout the book. If you want your feedback included in a future version, take the Goal Survey at TheDebMethod.com/GoalSurvey.

How to Use *Your Goal Guide*

Use this book in the way it best serves you.

Whether you need to make a major life-change or minor adjustments to your lifestyle—and even if you know what you want—go through Part 1 to set goals. It's your guide through the three phases of The D*E*B Method. Return to this section whenever you feel the need to refresh or reboot your plan. Use Part 2, which has tips for a successful trip, as well as the resources in the Appendices to stay on schedule and on track.

Oil Changes: Use the same time frame for reviewing and rebooting your goals as you use for servicing your car. Oil changes are recommended every six months. While you should review your goals regularly, try to place a minimum of three months between goal reboots.

Of course, there are exceptions to every rule: life changes (you have to move), plans change (you didn't get the job), things change (a surprise personal or professional opportunity gets thrown in your lap), and you have to make adjustments. However, if you change your destination every week or even every month, just because you are not getting where you want to go fast enough, you'll find yourself frustrated and stalled. Don't panic. Give your plans a chance and give yourself a break.

Road Trip Survival Kit

To successfully plan and complete your goals, you need:

- Pen and paper, notebook, or dedicated computer document

    ◦ There are a lot of free-writing exercises throughout the book. You need to have a designated location to write them all down

    ◦ You may also want a separate journal

    ◦ Optional: Poster board or portfolio folder and other supplies for creating and keeping your Trip Map

- A calendar

    ◦ To make a change, you need to make the time. A calendar—paper, electronic, or both—keeps you organized and on schedule

- A timer

    ◦ It's the best tool for tracking work time, break time, and brainstorming time. And the best part is everyone has one on their mobile phone, which for most people is never too far away

- Computer, tablet, and/or smartphone

    ◦ This is essential for research and outreach

    ◦ Tip: A portable keyboard is a must for those working on the go

- Items related to your goals

    ◦ You will need specific resources based on what you need in order to achieve your goals

- ○ It can be electronic, educational, or interpersonal and involve supplies, vendors, and so on

- ○ This includes books, websites, videos, podcasts, courses, etc.

- The desire to make a change

Planning goals, like planning the perfect road trip, takes time, energy, and effort. When you make the commitment and do the work, the road ahead will be much smoother.

Throughout this book, I will be your goal guide and project catalyst. I will help you figure out what you want and break down your goals into doable parts. Combine that with strategies for success, and you are headed on the road trip of your dreams. Trust me. And trust yourself. The time and energy will be worth it.

PART 1
Setting Up Your Road Trip

Where did you go on your last road trip? And what made that experience so special?

Was everything planned? Or did you jump in the car and go? I'm guessing it was probably a mixture. Even spontaneity—a.k.a. breaks for food and fun—works better when time is carved out for it.

I grew up in the Chicago suburbs, so I went on a lot of nearby adventures when I was a kid. These were mostly forays into the city to be a tourist or drives into Michigan to see family. As a teen and young adult, road trips became more of a rite of passage: driving to college, visiting friends, and having mini-adventures.

What is the minimum length of a road trip? Does a two-and-a-half-hour drive count? I figure anywhere you can get to between meals is more transit than road trip. But day trips have their place. Regardless of distance, in a perfect world—and in the goal-setting world—the journey should be as much fun as the destination.

My longest road trip was the one that led me to Los Angeles in my twenties when my mom and I tailgated across the country in two cars. The drive took us ten days and included a variety of joys: we played tourist, made new friends, ate good food. We also had more than our fair share of challenges. For instance, a massive thunderstorm delayed our initial departure, I got a speeding ticket before getting on the first highway, and there was a snowstorm in the panhandle of Texas, which shut down our direct route and took us hundreds of miles out of our way. Plus, each of our cars broke down in a different city—mine in Oklahoma, Mom's on the highway in Dallas on Christmas Eve; we were stranded for four hours before a cab driver—on his first day of work—stopped to help. And just when we thought we were in the home stretch, we were hit with three hours of bumper-to-bumper traffic.

We made it to Los Angeles exhausted, but ecstatic. We were ready for our next adventure to begin.

* * *

I have taken plenty of day trips and road trips; I've also been on a number of goal trips. As an adult, I worked more than a dozen jobs in two different states and have had too many interests, hobbies, and side projects to count. I've maintained relationships and friendships, and dealt with family dynamics and life drama, all while aspiring to find the perfect work-life balance. Many of my friends, clients, and contemporaries have had their own version of this story. What's yours? And more importantly, what do you want your story to be?

I believe everyone deserves to be happy in some, if not every, part of their lives. We all have responsibilities, and that means working to earn money to support the life you have.

But what about the life you want?

If you are already doing something you love, can you find a way to make it better, more lucrative, more impactful?

If you don't have a job or career that you love, is it feasible to change paths and find one?

And if switching jobs isn't an option, can you create something in your life that you enjoy, that gives you hope, that may lead to something bigger and better down the line?

That's what I am here to help you figure out.

In Part 1, we will plan your road trip. First, we'll start by setting your sights on something—anything—that will make you happy. This can be an ideal life, an ultimate goal, your GoalTopia. In the next phase, we will do some research to pinpoint exactly where that is and what that means to you. Finally, we will brainstorm, organize, and strategize in order to create a plan—a roadmap—that gets you where you want to go.

In this wonderful age of technology and accessibility, trying new things and shifting careers is easier than ever. Since we have an influx of options, we find ourselves constantly re-evaluating our professional—and personal—situations. However, only some people make changes voluntarily. Many wait until they are forced into action due to circumstance (their job is being eliminated, they're in an unhealthy work environment, they have to move), choice (they want to start or grow their own business, it's time for a career change, they want to have better work-life balance), or both (they want and need to increase their income).

Regardless of the motivation behind it, the best way to assure a successful trip is to come up with a roadmap ahead of time to get you to your destination. There will still be joys as well as bumps in the road, but at least you will know where you are going. And in terms of setting goals, that's the most important part. You can't get what you want unless you know what you want.

Are you ready to take your next road trip?

Let's start planning.

SECTION 1
Determine Where You Want to Go: Your Mission

Do you know what you want? Great. Not sure? That's fine, too. We'll figure it out together.

Setting goals is just like planning a road trip. You want to figure out where you want to go (your happy place, your ideal life, your GoalTopia) and decide what vehicle (mission or desire) will take you there.

So what road trip most appeals to you? For what purpose?

- Going to the mountains to enjoy nature, have an adventure, and challenge yourself to explore bigger and better things

- Heading to an amusement park to ride roller coasters, get a little dizzy, and enjoy the ups and downs

- Going to the city to see your name in lights and receive the recognition you deserve for being a knowledgeable force in your industry

- Spending time at the beach, relaxing, and realizing there's more to life than work

The same theory applies to planning your goals. You not only need to figure out what you want, but give some thought to how doing so will improve your life and the lives of those around you.

What do you want to do? Why?

- Find a new job in order to feel more fulfilled in your career

- Find a new job because your current position is being eliminated or you want to get out of a hostile work environment

- Start or grow your business to earn more money

- Share your expertise so others can learn from your experience

- Make a drastic change—or a series of minor ones—to improve your quality of life

- Prioritize relationships and family, so you have a happier personal life

- Increase your income to create financial independence

- All of the above? Some of these goals may fulfill more than one purpose

Once you know what you want and what drives you, then all of the long- and short-term goals you set will build upon each other to help you achieve it. Think of your GoalTopia as your focal point. In order to reach that or any destination, you need to decide exactly where you are going, what vehicle to take (mission), and what type of fuel (goals) will get you there.

In the first five chapters of *Your Goal Guide*, I will walk you through a variety of techniques, mainly writing exercises, to help you figure out where you want to go and why.

Chapter 1
Visualize Your GoalTopia

In order to get what you want, you need to know
what you want. You should also be able to see it.
And if you can hear it, feel it, and imagine it, that's
even better.

You know how attitude is everything, right? Positive thinking
is like magic. So is negative thinking, by the way. A bad or
stressed aura brings with it a cloud of darkness. You won't get
any of that in this book. Only positive vibes here.

The point is this: you are more likely to achieve something
if you are able to visualize it happening to you in the present
tense. To solidify that intention, you also want to create a visual
representation of your desired reality. This could be anything
from a billion-dollar check made out to you to a picture of your
happy family. Eyes on the prize.

But we're getting a little ahead of ourselves. Let's start
by figuring out your definition of GoalTopia, a.k.a. your
ultimate goal.

GoalTopia

When you think about the life you want, what comes to mind?
What are you doing? Where are you sitting? Who is with you?
Do you have a happy and balanced life?

Most people have a dream in their head, something they've always wanted to do. This desire may have been sparked during their childhood. It could be altered over time, but that glimmer of an idea—a perfect destination, their GoalTopia—started very long ago.

Here's mine. When I was a teenager, I decided I was going to write the Great American Novel. I'd planned this idealistic writer's life. When I grew up, I would rent out a cabin in Vermont, close out the world, and write. This idea still made sense to me throughout high school and college, since I wrote mostly fiction. I was even accepted into a creative writing program, but, instead, I took the more logical route. I got a degree in journalism. Still, I still had a creative itch and maintained that I would live that writer-life someday. I took screenwriting classes and have participated in National Novel Writing Month (a.k.a. NaNoWriMo) several times.

Well, here's how life laughed at my plans. I got my first freelance article assignment a week after I completed the first draft of my first screenplay. Not long after, I was writing columns and doing feature articles for a hip magazine aimed for college-aged through twenty-something readers. Over time, my desire to write a novel became less important than writing a non-fiction book. I self-published two of those, before getting the opportunity to go the traditional route with this one.

My point is this: Your dreams may pivot. They may even change. But there must be a kernel of something you've always wanted to do that makes it into your adult mind, if not your adult life.

What Do You Want?

Go back in time. Think about those things that have stuck with you—the activities you did as a kid and thought about pursuing—the ideas that roll around in your head and show themselves every now and again. Now's the time to take them out to play.

Were you the entrepreneur who sold not just lemonade, but snacks, door-to-door? Do you get annoyed every time you see someone else introduce an invention or service you thought up years ago? Do you dream about running your own business?

Were you a member of the art clubs in high school, but detoured to a more stable career? Have you always wondered what would happen if you had pursued creative arts? Is what stopped you then still stopping you now?

Did you volunteer, lead a book club, or bake lemon meringue pies for friends and family? Are you still doing some version of that? Would you like to?

Maybe the life you want has nothing to do with the life you have. And that's okay, too. This chapter is all about one question: What do you want? And only you can answer it.

Road Trip Exercise 1A: GoalTopia

Take out your notebook or open a dedicated computer document. At the top of the page, write "GoalTopia." Underneath, write "GoalTopia 1." You can also use the worksheet at the back of this book.

What's Your Ultimate Dream, Goal, or Desired Accomplishment?

- Are you a bestselling author, flourishing creative, or sought-out expert?

- Do you own a successful business?

- Are you excelling in your current role at work? Getting promoted?

- Are you pursuing a different career?

- Do you have a happy relationship, lots of money, and a well-balanced life? What does that look like?

Write down the first thing that comes to mind.

Done? Great.

Now, give it some thought. Meditate. Set a timer for fifteen minutes. Close your eyes, clear your mind, and let your thoughts wander. Try not to fall asleep. But if you do, no worries. The timer should wake you.

Visualization Hack: Meditation

Meditation itself has many versions. If you live in a big city like I do, you may find a studio that offers a variety of meditation practices like guided meditation, crystal and aroma therapy, or sound healing. You can also find a variety of guided meditations to listen to online or through an app. *I like the Insight Timer app; it has more than 25,000 free guided meditations.*

The simplest way to meditate is to sit comfortably, close your eyes, breathe naturally, and focus on your breath. This enables you to clear your mind, leaving room for contemplation and reflection. Meditation reduces stress, increases clarity, and re-energizes you. These are all valuable attributes as you figure out your GoalTopia.

However, many people have their own version of meditation that is way more active and effective. If sitting still as you ponder doesn't suit you, there are alternatives.

Divert your concentration: Take a walk, play video games, do a puzzle.

Take part in an activity: Exercise, do the dishes, fold laundry.

Sleep: Put the question "What do I want?" in your head before you go to sleep, and see what comes to mind in the morning.

Meditation, like many actions, is about trial and error. Explore different forms to discover what works best for you.

Time's up.

Write your next header: "GoalTopia: Take 2."

Answer the question again: What's your ultimate dream, goal, or accomplishment?

Write it down.

If necessary, repeat this process a few more times. You picked up this book for a reason. I'm guessing it's because you know you need a life-change. You also probably know what you want to do, but it may take a little time to bring it to the forefront of your mind. If need be, give yourself an extra day, or two, tops. You don't want to go into overthinking mode.

Review Your List

Once you are happy with your potential GoalTopias, read through the list.

Do you see similarities? Is everything the same? What keeps popping up? This could have to do with your job or career, company, industry, family, health, wealth, lifestyle. It may be a combination of all of the above.

After some consideration, from your list, identify the GoalTopia—or combination of GoalTopias—you want to focus on and write it down under the header: "Ultimate GoalTopia."

Case Studies

This first case study has a few different versions of GoalTopias, but her ideas share a common element.

Career Change

Cynthia likes, but doesn't love, her job. Her biggest frustration is that due to budgetary constraints, her salary level is not commensurate with her knowledge and experience. She knows she needs to start her own business or, preferably, get a new job at another company.

GoalTopia 1: Quit my job and work for people who appreciate me and compensate accordingly

GoalTopia 2: Become CEO of a Fortune 500 Company

GoalTopia 3: Have enough money to not worry about bills

GoalTopia 4: Be happy and healthy doing what I love and enjoy quality time with my family

GoalTopia 5: Start my own successful business

These ideals are interrelated, so they can be easily combined.

Ultimate GoalTopia: Find a position with a growing company—or create one—where I can share my knowledge and be a productive, well-compensated member and eventual leader of the team; be happy, healthy, and wealthy; and have nice work-life balance.

In this next one, these GoalTopias are all over the place:

Reboot

Travis left his job in the entertainment business last year due to health issues. He worked his way up from being a production assistant and knows practically everything about being behind-the-scenes in the film and TV industry. He has been doing some contract work, but really wants to develop his side projects that teach up-and-comers what they need to know to survive in Hollywood.

GoalTopia 1: Find a new industry niche, so I can continue to work/earn

GoalTopia 2: Write my memoir to share my stories, while teaching wannabes and entertaining fans of the shows I worked on

GoalTopia 3: Relaunch my podcast

GoalTopia 4: Launch my series of workshops/retreats

GoalTopia 5: Be healthy

Travis wants to find a new specialty, while sharing stories from his old one.

Ultimate GoalTopia: Get the education and training I need to carve out a new industry niche while developing projects that enable me to share stories from my old one. And be healthy and wealthy to boot.

And then there are GoalTopias where the business element only serves to support a happy lifestyle.

Happy Life

Olivia started a consulting company about a year ago after she was laid off from her job. She works in a niche business, so finding clients that fit can be a challenge. Olivia wants to have a successful business, but the GoalTopia she wants is the happy life that goes with it.

GoalTopia 1: Financial freedom so I can do what I want

GoalTopia 2: Buy a house

GoalTopia 3: Travel the world

GoalTopia 4: Be happy

GoalTopia 5: Have an interesting career or business

In Olivia's scenario, a successful business is secondary to happiness.

Ultimate GoalTopia: Make lots more money so I can spend it on a house and travel while doing work that I like and makes me happy.

When you go through this exercise, focus on the goals you keep thinking about. The ideas you keep coming back to deserve thoughtful consideration, no matter how extreme they seem.

Whether you aim to be the go-to expert in your field, run a successful business, or just live a happy life, it's up to you. It's your GoalTopia. You are going to put a lot of effort into this process. Strive for what you want!

More GoalTopias

Here are some additional examples of GoalTopias, based on my clients, my community, and the Goal Survey.

- Be a world-renowned speaker

- Publish my novels and market and sell them

- Become an award-winning screenwriter

- Work every day at a job that I love, where I am paid well and feel like a contributing member of the team

- Get promoted

- Become the boss

- Quit my job and start my own business

- Quit my job and pursue a new career

- Earn a living doing something I love

- Turn my hobby into a business

- Finish the projects I start and get them out into the world

- Have a life outside of work

- Run a marathon

- Go back to school

- Earn my doctorate

- Have my skills and talents be recognized

- Share my story so others can learn from my experience

- Live without financial stress

- Own a home

- Take vacations twice a year

- Become healthy
- Stay healthy
- Find happiness

Remember, your goals will evolve as the things in your life change. However, for the purpose of this process, the GoalTopia you choose should reflect what matters to you most right now.

Visual Representation

Now that you know where you want to go, let's have a little fun. Figure out what your GoalTopia looks like. Create something visual: a drawing, a collage, or a mock-up on the computer. You will use this as a visual cue to remind you of what you are working toward.

Are you artistic? Draw a picture.

Want to go old-school? Make a collage. Cut out pics from a magazine or newspaper and mock them up.

Are you, like me, *not* artistically inclined? Go the electronic route. Find photos online and use an image-creation program. Online graphics tools, like Canva, enable you to easily upload and combine photos.

Visual Representation Hack: Alternative Visual Cues

Not one for arts and crafts? Pick an item that represents what you are trying to achieve and keep it on your desk or somewhere else in your line of sight.

- Is financial stability the goal? Write yourself a check for a million dollars

- Looking to advance in your career? Print out an "Employee of the Year" card to keep in your wallet

- For work-life balance, a postcard of the beach should do the trick

- If you want to visualize a physical move, get a pen, shirt, or coffee mug from that ideal location

Whatever the object, it doesn't need to make sense to passersby. That's kind of the point. It needs to only be meaningful to you.

As far as what you can create, the options are endless. Here are some examples:

Do you want your name to be associated with those who are highly respected in your industry? Find a newspaper or magazine (online or in print) that has a "Top Ten" list of people in your field. Add your name and photo to it.

Is your GoalTopia to create a must-have product? Make a mock-up of a photo of your product being sold in stores. Bonus points if you add a celebrity endorsement.

Want to launch a successful business? Create an image of what your website would look like. Add an award or stamp of approval for good measure.

Do you aim to speak in front of large groups? Place a photo of yourself on a stage giving a keynote speech to a packed audience.

Want to be on top of the *New York Times* Bestseller list? Take the current list and write your name and book title right at the top.

Is your GoalTopia to be financially stable and happy? Decide what that looks like. Are you relaxing on vacation? Having fun with your family and friends? Opening the door to your new home?

Your visualization is just that—yours. It can be anything you want it to be.

Road Trip Exercise 1B: Visual Representation

Create your visual representation. Once you finish it:

On Paper

Place the original in your notebook on the page after your GoalTopia exercise.

Or

Take a photo, upload it, and insert it into your dedicated computer document.

On Computer

Save the image.

Insert it into your dedicated computer document.

Or

Print out two copies. One for your notebook. The other for your Trip Map.

Trip Map

Take your original visual representation or printed copy—along with your statement of Ultimate GoalTopia—and frame it, laminate it, or otherwise protect it, and add it to your Trip Map.

Your Trip Map is where you will compile—and look at—the visual cues you create relating to your goal trip. As your Trip Map grows, take pictures of it to store on your phone and keep on hand.

You are probably thinking you need to get a large whiteboard or corkboard, or an actual map, and put it up over a big chunk of your office. While those are viable options, your Trip Map does not need to be huge. It doesn't even have to be a map, though it can be. And it only needs to be visible to you.

I keep my Trip Map on the back of a two-foot by three-foot canvas frame in my office. It is located right behind my computer and visible to me at all times, but I can easily turn it around if someone is coming by and I want to keep it private. If you have limited space or your office is mobile, get a letter-sized portfolio folder which has a solid cover and clear pocket pages.

This map will serve as a hub of visual reminders of what you are working toward. It's an extremely powerful part of your road trip planning.

Chapter 2
Write Your Current Biography

You are a combination of your personal and
professional histories.
Embrace what makes you unique and use it to propel
yourself forward.

Before heading off on any trip, you need to take an inventory
of where you are: your location, current work situation, and
lifestyle. You also want to look at your resources. For a road
trip, that means looking at your car (will it get you where you
want to go?), your budget (where can you afford to stay during
your travels?), and how much time you can take. For a goal trip,
you need to look at your skills and specialties in order to see
what translates into something you can pack to take with you.

Let's say you want to quit your job to become a chef. If you are
already a prolific home cook, then you are off to a good start,
although you will need more education and training. If the only
appliances you use are your toaster oven and pressure cooker,
you have a way to go in amassing skills. It's still possible, but
the journey will be of a greater distance.

Want to climb the corporate ladder? You need to identify what
skills you already have that make you the ideal candidate.

Want to start a podcast? What from your background will make
for good content?

Want to grow your business or start a side hustle? Do you have
the sales, marketing, or customer service chops to leverage to
help you succeed?

Writing your biography will remind you of what you have done and what your capabilities are.

Your Biography

A bio is a document which runs anywhere from a few lines, to a couple paragraphs, to a page in length. This is where you share your accomplishments, experience, and expertise, along with your strengths and values. Unlike a résumé, it's in narrative form and should be written in your tone and style, showing some personality along with your professional background. It's the public's first impression of you. And it's a good way to remind yourself of all you have done and what you want to achieve.

You Are Here

Most people find writing their bio extremely challenging. I know writers who have literally spent hours upon hours writing and rewriting their biographies. Don't do that. Yes, you want something good, but you don't want to derail your road trip prep by getting stuck in Chapter 2.

Remember, you can revise your biography at any time. As you aspire toward your goals, you will likely need your bio for your business, website or blog, byline, query, etc. However, for the purposes of your road trip, don't get stuck on the words. Do your best to capture who you are now.

To assist you, I have some simple tricks to make this process easier.

Go to a Networking Event

Whether it's a breakfast mixer or evening event, networking schmooze-fests have the sole purpose of encouraging their attendees to meet a lot of people in a short period of time. Think of it as speed-dating with professional interest. Come to think of it, some cities even do speed-networking events. That's even better.

When you've spent an hour or so introducing yourself to a bunch of new people, your background will be in easy-recall mode. Write notes as soon as feasible after the networking experience. Jot down the highlights or repeat your introduction to yourself via voice memo.

Ask Friends

Stumped as to which of your characteristics and experiences stand out? Ask your friends and peers. People you know and trust will offer a unique, unbiased perspective. Make sure your questions are open-ended.

For instance, ask:

- Do you remember your first impression of me?

- How would you describe me to someone else?

- What was your favorite/funniest/most-serious business/ client/project experience with me?

Give people the opportunity to talk about you to you. They will definitely come up with stories that didn't occur to you. And they may even want you to return the favor and help with their own bio.

Research Yourself

If you do no other prep for writing your bio, try this.

You likely have several versions of your résumé from over the years floating around. You may even have written a bio for your blog, company website, or LinkedIn.

Gather any and every version of your bio and résumé that exists. Search for old versions in your filing cabinet, on your computer, or online. Print out any computer documents or screenshots. Once you have everything together, read them.

Done? Awesome. Now put them away.

I want you to start with a clean slate. You can double-check the dates later. This research will help you paint a picture of the complete current version of you.

Road Trip Exercise 2A: Biography Highlights

Go to the next page in your dedicated notebook or document, and title it, "Current Bio." Or use the worksheet in the back of the book.

Fill in the Following:

Employment History. Put an asterisk next to any career highlights. We want to pinpoint any outstanding work experience.

Education, Organizations, and Certifications. Note any leadership roles and local groups, whether or not they relate to work.

Successes. List any awards as well as your proudest accomplishments.

Strengths. Strengths need to go beyond what makes you good at your job. Also note what makes you a good friend/spouse/boss/employee/parent/child/person.

Challenges. You hate when they ask the "weakness" question at job interviews. Here's your chance to change the language. What was your greatest challenge at work, and how did you prevail?

Skills. Can you bake a soufflé without it falling? Are you able to recall every book you've ever read? Can you do yoga on a standup paddleboard? These may sound like cooking, reading, and athletic skills, but I think these show patience, memory, and balance. When listing your skills, think outside the box.

Personal Details or Anecdotal Information. This is where you can list any cool stories that didn't make it into the previous categories.

You are probably thinking this is *too much information.* And it is a lot. But it's better to have too many details than too few. You have more to work with that way.

Road Trip Exercise 2B: Current Biography

Take the information you charted out and turn the high points into a bio written in the third person. For professional reasons, it's good to have short (two- to three-line), medium (two- to three-paragraphs), and long (one page) versions of your biography. For this exercise, aim for 150 to 300 words. It should be something you would find in a pitch letter or on a book jacket, promotional material, or website "About" page.

Keep in mind that every bio is different, just as every person is different. The point is to enjoy the process and let your personality come out via your words.

> **Bio Hack: Investigate What's Out There**
>
> Go online and find ten bios that are in or adjacent to your area of expertise. You want a mix of different types of bios, so be sure to include at least one or two industry celebs. Read through them and make a list of what you do and *do not* like about each one. Of course, you don't want to copy someone else's experience. Use this for inspiration of what to do and not do.

Biography Starters

Still stuck? Just fill in the blanks:

> **Professional Bio**
>
> A (current position), (name) is known for (fill in the blank). After (time) working at (job), he/she decided to take his/her aptitude for (skill) and (did this accomplishment). He/she also (did this). A (characteristic), (Name) is a (professional groups/leadership) and excels in (more skills). In his/her downtime, he/she (does this). (Optional: personal trivia.)

Or

Impassioned Bio

(Name) enjoys (fill in the blank), which is something that shows in all he/she does. For instance, (example) and (example). (Name) currently does (position) at (company), where he/she is responsible for (fill in the blank). With (personality traits), he/she is determined to (fill in the blank). A (character traits), (name) also likes to (personal something or other).

Or

Hobby Bio

On any given day, (Name) can be found (fill in the blank). A long-time (doer of activity), he/she also enjoys (this), (that), and (the other thing). (Name) currently does (position) at (company), where he/she is responsible for (fill in the blank). (Name) truly shines when (fill in the blank). He/she can't wait for (blank).

Write a few versions of your bio until you settle on one you like. Note your favorite as *final* in your notebook.

Chapter 3
Predict Your Future Biography

Don't just visualize yourself leading a happy and
successful life, put it into words.

The next step in this process is to figure out your future. Take
the distance from where you are to where you want to go and
fill in the blanks.

Since you've determined which of your experiences can be
translated and taken on your goal trip, identify what additional
skills, education, and relationships you need to pick up or
develop along the way. Also, think about what you want to have
accomplished during your journey when you look back.

Detail your personal as well as professional aspirations in your
future biography.

Your Future Biography

Before you take a crack at your future bio, look at your ultimate
goal and visual representation from Chapter 1. *If it's not
somewhere nearby, you missed a step.* Now imagine what
your biography will say once you get to GoalTopia. Use items
from your current bio, incorporate your aspirations and fill in
the blanks.

This exercise is twofold. Your narrative will reinforce the
visualization exercise from the first chapter. It also serves as a

mileage check. When you see the distance between your current life and your future, you can begin to chart your course.

Of course, the details will likely change—your real future hasn't happened yet—but that is going to occur throughout this process. It's important to remember as you go through this book that this is supposed to be fun. Sure, you want to take this seriously, but these are creative exercises. Keep your tone light and your options open.

Where Is There?

Your future biography should reflect your ideal persona, the person you are striving to become once you reach your yet-to-be-determined destination. While you may have some idea of what getting there will entail, you'll still have to do some legwork.

Here are some things you can do to fill in the blanks.

Research

The obvious first step is to do research online. Search your areas of interest and ideal jobs. Watch some YouTube videos. Do a job search for the position to which you aspire in order to check on skills and qualifications.

Beyond looking at traditional resources, seek out relevant entertainment. Read a book that takes place in your desired field. Watch a movie, be it documentary, biography, drama, or comedy. Or, if you really want to feel motivated, watch something inspirational. That underdog-succeeding-against-all-odds story never gets old.

Much like you would read a travel guide while planning your vacation, look to people who have done this work before. These can be stories from real people or the adventures of fictional characters.

Go Undercover

Another way to figure out the education, skills, and temperament necessary to work in a certain industry is to go to an event. It probably helps to know someone—or have a friend of a friend—who does something similar, but it isn't always necessary. Ask to tag along to their next industry mixer. Another option is to volunteer at a conference or workshop. People putting on events will usually welcome some extra help.

Surrounded by potential peers, you'll learn a lot about what you need to do to imagine that future and see if it's a fit for you.

Be sure to exchange business cards or contact info with the people you meet and connect with them on LinkedIn and any other social networks. You'll want to reach out to them in the future.

Phone a Friend

Having trouble pinpointing your future? Ask a childhood friend or a pal from college what you used to talk about accomplishing in your youth. A simple reminder could open a plethora of possibilities.

Road Trip Exercise 3A: Future Biography Highlights

Go to the next page in your dedicated notebook or document and title it, "Future Bio." Or use the worksheet in the back of the book.

Fill in the Following

Future Work Experience. Are you making lateral moves into a different industry, moving up the ladder in your current work environment, or doing something new? Note some of the positions you will take. This may also include volunteer positions and fun pursuits.

Education, Organizations, and Certifications. List any necessary education, certifications, and leadership roles, as well as local and national groups to join.

Successes. If you have your eye on certain awards or dream accomplishments, this is where to include them.

New Skills. As you work toward your ultimate goal, you will need to acquire some new skills. List some of those future talents.

Personal Ambitions. What do you want your personal life to look like in the future?

This is basically a creative writing exercise wrapped up in an alternate reality. Take as much time as you want or need to fill in some of these blanks.

Road Trip Exercise 3B: Future Biography

Use the information you came up with to write your future bio. Figure out a likely scenario. Then, amp it up a lot. It's invigorating to shoot for the stars. Just base it in reality.

Write Three Versions of Your Biography

One year from now.

Five years from now.

Ten years from now.

If you want to do only one of these, write the five-year version.

Remember, possibilities are limited only by your imagination. And reality is limited only by what you are willing and able to do to get to where you want to go.

Future Bio Hack: Add Your Headshot

No bio is complete without a photo. Add your pic next to your future biographies as another visualization cue. Associating how you look with what you want to do will help it sink in that this life-change is not just possible, it's probable.

Future Biography Starters

Need some inspiration? Fill in the blanks:

Business Bio

(Name) is the founder and CEO of (company). After years of (doing this), he/she launched (business) and became the fastest growing (doer of this). He/she (did something revolutionary) and has been listed as (names of honors). (Name) has homes in New York, Los Angeles, and Europe, and vacations on his/her private island with his/her family every summer. An avid fan of (something), he/she plans to (do this) next.

Or

Author Bio

The author of (titles), (Name)'s (title) has been on the *New York Times* Bestseller list for the past forty weeks. He/she got her start (doing this), and after (crossroads), decided to pursue his/her passion for (subject) full-time. (Name) speaks regularly (here, here, and here), is a regular contributor to (publications), and is often the guest expert on (TV show). Watch for his/her next book, (title), to be released next fall.

Or

Hobby Bio

(Name) enjoys/does (fill in the blank). When he/she was (age), he/she began (doing this). (Name) spends his/her days (doing this), nights (doing that), and has become the (spokesperson) for (topic). In addition to (how expert is known), he/she also does (this), (that), and (the other thing). (Name) has achieved something to which many aspire: good health, happiness, and a well-balanced life.

Although the details may change, your future bio will help you focus on what you want your life to look like once you reach GoalTopia. Be sure to add a copy of it to your Trip Map.

Chapter 4
Create Your Mission Statement

When you work on anything, do so with purpose.

Your mission statement is a summary of your goals and values, as well as the driving force behind them. It's the vehicle that takes you on your road trip. Furthermore, once you know your mission, you are able to set long- and short-term goals that reflect it.

Keep in mind, you can have a mission statement for yourself, your business, and each of your projects.

For this journey, you want to create a professional or personal mission statement for your trip to GoalTopia.

The Mission Statement

If you've ever worked in business, your company likely had a mission statement to empower employees and inspire related activities.

If you ever met with a life coach or went to career counseling, you may have been encouraged to create a personal mission statement.

The destination mission statement, which is what you're going to create, is more of a combination. You want to stay specific to a tangible goal while incorporating your beliefs and experience.

The Value

Since your mission statement combines who you are (your biography) and what you stand for (ethics) with your purpose (ultimate goal), you've done a lot of this legwork already. So it is really a matter of putting all the pieces together, mixing them up, and adding one more.

To be successful, the things you do and create ultimately need to serve others. If you do something just for yourself, that's an audience of one.

When creating your mission statement, identify the value—it can be for entertainment, education, wellness, business, beauty, etc.—as well as who it will serve. That will be your driving force.

Road Trip Exercise 4: Mission Statement

Go to the next page in your dedicated notebook or document and title it, "Mission Statement." Or use the worksheet in the back of the book.

As you pull this information together, feel free to look back on your biography notes. You want to be as concise as possible in answering these questions.

Who You Are + What You Want = Your Mission Statement

Who are you? What is your work, education, and personal background as it relates to your ultimate goal?

What are your values? What ideals and principles are important to you?

What are your unique qualities? What characteristics, talents, and skills not only describe you, but define you?

What do you ultimately want? What is your goal?

Who does it serve and why? What is the value to others? Note: This still works for personal goals. For instance, if your goal is to develop a healthier lifestyle, that's still of value to your family and those around you as much as it is for yourself.

Mission Statement Hack: Directed Journaling

Having trouble figuring out your mission statement? Jump ahead to Chapter 6 and read about Directed Journaling. The concept is to use free-writing to figure out pretty much anything. So, you may need to spend some time journaling in order to arrive at your mission statement.

Once you've gathered the information you need, create your mission statement. It will vary depending on whether your primary focus for your goal trip is personal or professional.

Mission Statement Fill-in-the-Blank

Professional. I am a (adjective) person who enjoys (talent) and excels at (skill) who wants to help (demographic) (do this) in order to (reason).

Personal. I am a (adjective) person who does (skill), enjoys (interest), and wants to do (action) in order to (do this).

You may need to write a few versions of your mission statement until you hit on the right one. But that's totally fine. You'll know when you've arrived at your mission.

Once you have your mission statement, add it to your Trip Map.

Remember, your mission statement doesn't have to be perfect and it will change over time. Select something that speaks to you in your current frame of mind as you plan this road trip.

Chapter 5

Turn Your Mission Statement into a Motto

Call it a motto, a slogan, or a tag line, it's you...
in shorthand.

If your mission statement is your vehicle, your motto is the nickname you have for it. Something short, simple, and memorable with a hint of affection. Your motto should say everything about who you are and what you are working toward in three to five words.

For the Job Seeker: I Know Things. (Whatever the topic, a reminder of what you're good at is really important for someone feeling underappreciated at the office.)

For the Entrepreneur: Building *this* for *that reason*. (For the solopreneur, side hustler, or CEO, go with a reminder of what you are creating and the purpose and people behind it.)

For the Expert: King/Queen of *Topic*. (Exercise, Food, Sports, Trivia, Technology.)

As I mentioned in Chapter 4, to be effective and productive, your goals should all relate to or reflect your mission. A motto is a shortened version of your mission statement, so you can use it as a barometer for making decisions that relate to your goals.

Motto as Compass

Once you get on the road to GoalTopia, you will see different tourist traps and roadside attractions—a.k.a. opportunities—that may deter you from your path. Some may benefit you, while others will not.

It also serves as a personal navigation device. As potential opportunities come your way, you can look to your mission to help you decide what does and does not make sense to pursue.

You may need to ask yourself:

- Does it serve my professional or personal mission?

- Will this job, assignment, or meeting help me move forward? Can it give me experience or connections?

- Will this be a fun diversion from my goals that will help me in other ways? Can I make new friends? Can it be a low-stress break? Or will it deter me from something more valuable?

- Will it take me on a wild goose chase and cost me time and/or money?

You will use your motto to assess what is in line with your goals, what has value in other ways, and what you need to avoid altogether.

My Motto Moment

My mission is to use my skills, experience, and passion for goal-setting to help individuals and businesses define, plan, and achieve their goals.

My motto is Goal-Setting Simplified. I look to those words whenever I create new content or review opportunities to expand my visibility and business.

I was recently asked to speak on a panel about women navigating the workplace. Although it's been several years since I worked at an office doing a typical day job, I certainly could speak on the subject. But I had to ask myself, "Would it serve my mission?" Possibly, but not in the same way other, more goal-centric or writing-focused panels would.

I gave it some consideration, and then looked at my calendar. The panel was scheduled for January. The early part of the year is the busiest in the goal-coaching space. So I had to decide whether it was worth blocking off time to prep and attend in January when I might be spreading myself too thin. As it turned out, a more ideal opportunity presented itself for that same day. I was glad I passed on something that did not fit my mission as it left me open for something that did.

Road Trip Exercise 5: Motto

Go to the next page in your dedicated notebook or document and title it, "Motto." Or use the worksheet in the back of the book.

Motto Planning

First, rewrite your mission statement at the top of the page.

Then, pull five to seven keywords from the goal in your mission statement.

Next, write out the first five ideas for mottos that come to mind.

Now write five more.

Look at your list. Put asterisks next to your three favorites.

Go do something. Get a glass of water, answer some email, do the dishes.

Alright. Look at your list again.

Does one of the three favorites stand out? Or do you need to write some more ideas?

Motto Hack: Adopt a Song

Think of your motto as your personalized theme song. It's the compass by which you will make decisions, so you want something that will stick in your head.

If you are having trouble coming up with a motto, borrow a song. One TV moment that has been stuck in my head for years is when on the TV show *Ally McBeal*, Ally's therapist, played by Tracey Ullman, tells her to come up with a theme song.

Your motto should energize you, motivate you. It should make you smile. So, if you can't come up with a motto, pick a favorite song that inspires the same sentiment as your mission statement.

Like with your mission statement, when you hit on the right motto, you will know it. And it will stick in your head in the best possible way. So much so, that you will rarely have to look at it. But keep it handy anyway.

Rewrite your motto at the bottom of the page, add it to your Trip Map, and put it in any other places where you will see it regularly. It will keep you focused. And, possibly, even make you smile.

Section 1 Rapid Review

Before you continue to the next section, make sure you have everything. You don't want to leave anything behind. Note: There's a review worksheet in the back of the book.

Do you have the following?

- Your idea of GoalTopia

- Your Current Biography

- Your Future Biography

- Your Mission Statement

- Your Motto

Are all your elements together in your notebook and on your Trip Map?

Are you psyched to move on?

Pack them up and take them to the next section.

SECTION 2
Explore Different Destinations: Your Options

Although you now know what your GoalTopia looks like, you are just getting started. With each ultimate goal comes infinite possibilities.

You want to take a road trip to a big city, but which one? In the United States, there are major cities in all directions: on both coasts, in the Midwest, and down South. And each one is different.

Your ideal future has you as a known expert in your industry. But how will that play out? Are you going to create content? In what format? Whatever your ideal location, there are countless specific destinations. You need to narrow it down.

So where are you headed? What's it going to be?

WHERE DO YOU WANT TO GO?

MOUNTAIN RESORT—WORK CHANGE

- NEW JOB
- NEW CAREER
- CLIMB THE CORPORATE LADDER

AMUSEMENT PARK—START A BUSINESS

- A SIDE BUSINESS, A NEW BUSINESS, OR PLANS TO GROW YOUR BUSINESS
- PRODUCT OR SERVICE

BIG CITY—EXPERT IN YOUR FIELD

- WRITE A BOOK
- START A BLOG, SHOW, OR PODCAST
- BECOME A KEYNOTE SPEAKER

BEACH—PURSUE PERSONAL GOALS

- CHANGE IN RELATIONSHIP, LOCATION, OR HOME
- MORE TIME FOR FAMILY, FRIENDS, DATING
- FIND A NEW HOBBY, HAVE FUN, GET HEALTHY

In the next five chapters of *Your Goal Guide*, I will take you
through the process of investigating different possibilities.
The legwork, which includes writing, research, and outreach,
will help you identify options. As a result, you will be able to
pinpoint a destination that serves your mission.

Chapter 6
Begin Directed Journaling

It's much easier to see solutions on the page than in your head.

Once you have zoomed in on what you want your life to become—your ideal *type* of location—you need to take the time to figure out where and what that is exactly.

My favorite solution for figuring out pretty much anything is a technique I developed called "Directed Journaling." This journaling with a twist helps to work through any sort of concept, decision, or problem.

Have you ever noticed how difficult it is to find solutions simply by jiggling things around in your head? This method is effective because, when you put your ideas in writing, you are able to look at them objectively, move things around, and determine the best course of action.

To do Directed Journaling, set up a series of short appointments with yourself to write down your thoughts—through a stream of consciousness—on a specific topic. This journaling can be narrative, a list, an outline, phrases, free-writing, drawing, or all of the above. The trick is to let everything out of your head, related to something specific—in this case your GoalTopia—and use that information to craft your plan. The secret is to not look at your brainstorms until after you've done them all. No editing, no worrying about repeating yourself. Just a pure, unadulterated brain dump.

The Power of the Journal

Like most writers, I started keeping a journal in elementary
school; we called them "diaries" at that age. However, the true
benefits of journaling as an emotional release didn't hit home
until high school. My creative writing teacher, Dr. Amberg,
assigned everyone to write at least five pages in their journal
each week. I usually wrote about twenty pages, but I had
classmates who could fill up an entire notebook in a week.
Our teacher never read what we wrote; he just checked our
page count.

Getting words out of your head and onto the page helps you
emotionally, logically, and, I would bet, physically. Writing
releases stress, and, when you get stress out of your body, you
tend to feel better.

Selecting Your Journal

I've said this before, but it deserves repeating. It does not
matter whether you keep your journal on a computer document
or you use pen and a physical notebook.

Here's what does matter:

Choose the medium you will actually use. Sure, studies
show that there is a certain brain connection when you write
with a pen. But if you are not a fan of handwriting, you are
never going to do it.

Keep all of your journal entries in the same place. Use
the document or notebook you designated for *Your Goal Guide*
or start a fresh journal.

If you choose to incorporate your Directed Journaling into *Your Goal Guide* notebook, write "Journal" or "DJ" along with the date at the top of each journal page you use. Then, to indicate your journaling sections, use mini Post-it tabs for a physical notebook and use navigation tabs for a digital notebook. This will enable you to easily reference your journal pages as you work through this book.

Through Directed Journaling, you will explore the potential paths, benchmarks, and action items that will help you achieve your ultimate goal.

Road Trip Exercise 6: Directed Journaling

Choose your journal and take out your calendar. While there is no worksheet for this, journaling prompts are also listed in Appendix A.

How Directed Journaling Works

In your calendar, schedule at least three—but ideally five or more—short (fifteen-minute) sessions for journaling. Schedule the first one for right after you read these instructions. This is focused time where you write out your thoughts, answering a specific question or series of questions. Think of it as free-writing or babbling on paper, no censoring or editing allowed.

Note: There will be other occasions to journal throughout this process, but try to get all of the sessions pertaining to this exercise done within the week.

When you do your Directed Journaling, depending on your journey, ask yourself questions such as:

- What do I want?

  ◦ A new job? A new career? A completely different path?

  ◦ What should I do? What excites me about making this change?

- Do I want to create or grow something?

  ◦ What? A business? A product? A service? What product? What service?

  ◦ What reasons do I have for creating, promoting, and pursuing this or any project?

  ◦ Why am I the ideal person to create it? How will it help others?

- Am I looking to become a known expert?

  ◦ What will set me apart?

  ◦ Writing a book? Starting a blog, video show, or podcast? Becoming a keynote speaker?

  ◦ All of the above? What's first?

- Do I need to make a life-change?

  ◦ What sort of life-change? What might make me happy?

  ◦ What are my options? What are the pros and cons of each?

- What does work-life balance look like?

  ◦ Change in relationship, location, or home?

  ◦ More time for family, friends, dating?

  ◦ Find a new hobby, have fun, get healthy?

Do not look at your journal entries until you've completed the entire exercise.

You may need to journal more than five times. So if you are still sorting things out and need more sessions, go for it. We'll get to next steps in Chapter 7.

Journaling Hack: Visual Brainstorming

There are multiple ways to keep a journal. Some people prefer to use a computer and others choose to write by pen. Whichever way you best express yourself—whatever comes most naturally—is how you should do your journaling.

Doodling. Some people are more visual by nature. If you are not a natural writer, or even if you are, you can incorporate sketches into your journaling. You may use them to illustrate the answers to your Directed Journaling questions, or they may be the answers themselves.

Mind Mapping. A mind map is a visual tool that helps with brainstorming. The concept is to put one idea in the center of the page and then expand on different facets by drawing lines and then connecting related ideas. Think of it as a tree with a different branch for each specific thought.

While you can use pen and paper for mind maps, there are also websites and apps. For more on mind mapping, as well as recommendations for tools (some free, some paid), check out MindMapping.com.

Journaling Hack: Audio Brainstorming

In most scenarios, there is no substitute for the written word. However, if recording audio or video will enable you to brainstorm better or more consistently, I am all for it. The only caveat is you must transcribe your audio to use with future exercises.

You have some choices.

Use a Voice-to-Text Solution. Most smartphone keyboards have a microphone to click on for this function. You talk and text comes out. You can also talk into Google Docs. Although voice-to-text software has improved vastly over the years, it is not always 100 percent accurate. But this is a brainstorm, so it does not need to be exact. As long as your ideas come across well enough for you to understand, it's fine.

Record and Transcribe. There are plenty of transcription services available. You send out your audio, and it comes back transcribed. Some of the online or automated solutions are free or offer free trials, but most, especially the ones that use people instead of software, come with a cost. You can also ask your network for recommendations of transcriptionists or virtual assistants who offer that service. Paying for those fifteen-minute audio brainstorms adds up. But the time you save may be worth it. If you go that route, you probably want the transcriber to be a stranger. You don't want friends transcribing your brainstorms, do you?

For self-transcription, my favorite tool is a web solution called Transcribe. Record your audio on your phone or a digital recorder, transfer it to your computer, and upload it. They also offer a paid transcription service, but I prefer to do it myself. You can play audio in your headphones and talk it out, though this is also not 100 percent accurate and may require some revision. Or type it in yourself, using their tools to slow it down and pause.

Feel free to go back to journaling at any time during your travel-planning your goal trip, or while you are at your destination. More on journaling in Chapter 19, when we get into keeping a travel log to track your progress.

You can even use journaling to help you with things that are unrelated to this journey.

- Have an amazing experience? Write it down so you can revisit it at will.

- Frustrated with a coworker, a family member, or a situation? Write it down to get it out of your head and your heart.

- See something incredible? Write it down so you can solidify the memory.

Remember, journaling pages are for you. As long as you keep them in a private place, anything goes.

Chapter 7
List Common Themes

Within the patterns of your journal entries, you'll find where your interests lie.

Did you do it? Did you tap into your stream of consciousness to identify numerous scenarios that could lead you to achieve GoalTopia? Have you exhausted a variety of possibilities?

If the answer is, "No," go back to Chapter 6 and complete a few more Directed Journaling sessions.

If the answer is, "Yes," please proceed.

However...

If you completed your most recent journal entry within the last hour, take a break first. Grab a cup of coffee. Listen to music. Do something that relaxes you. I want you to approach this next exercise with a fresh perspective.

The Theme's the Thing

Just as you previously identified similarities while creating your mission statement and motto, we're going to home in on the commonalities—the theme, the dominant subject—of your journal entries in this chapter.

The reason you are not supposed to look at your journaling until you've done a complete brain dump is so you approach all of your ideas objectively. It's the same reason writers are told not to edit their work until after they've completed a draft. They get caught up in the details—going down a rabbit hole—and never quite get to the end. They don't see the complete picture.

When you give yourself the time to fully explore what could be and then review everything objectively, you'll be in a better position to identify what truly holds your interest. Pinpointing an exciting destination will keep you motivated as you plan and eventually take your road trip to GoalTopia.

Unlock Your Vehicle

Through identifying common themes in your journal, you'll find the key—the specifics—to start your goal trip.

Need to change your employment situation? You should be able to determine whether you need to find a new position at your current company, make a lateral move to a different company, or explore another career path.

Looking to start a business? This will help you home in on your industry or specialty, as well as what type of business: service or product, online or offline, full-time or side hustle.

Want to become known as an expert? Discover the best way to showcase your knowledge, whether it's through a book, a podcast, social media, public speaking, or a combination of approaches.

Do you want a more balanced life? Identify what balance means, what's holding you back, and which changes you need to make to your current situation. This could be related to your home, family, friends, or yourself.

Road Trip Exercise 7: Common Themes

Go to the next page in your dedicated notebook or document and title it, "Common Themes." Or use the worksheet in the back of the book.

Seek Overlaps and Omissions

Read through the first day of your journal entries. Then, jot down five things that stand out.

Repeat this for each of your journal days.

Now, compare your lists.

- What ideas showed up on most days? Every day?

- Are there any obvious omissions?

- What did you learn about yourself?

> **Common Theme Hack: Recalibrate**
>
> If you are still having trouble pinpointing where to go from here, try this: Take a break, reread your journal entries from start to finish, and then look at your lists again. You may want to journal some more, and that's fine too.

To give you an idea of what you should be looking for in your entries, here are a couple of case studies.

Side Hustle: Food Fan

Bob has a pretty good life. He's a single father who has shared custody of his two kids and has a well-paying corporate day job. But he wants to start a side hustle to bring in extra money and have a little fun with his kids. He is a great home cook and loves to entertain, and he is trying to pass that on to his kids. In GoalTopia, he has some sort of mini food empire. His motto is, "Food, Family, Fun," but he still doesn't know how that translates to a business.

The highlights from his journal entries went like this:

- Day 1: Should I open a food truck? It might be fun to do with the kids, but no. Should I open a restaurant? What do I know about restaurants? Money pit. I'll stick with the day job. But I do need to do something with my homemade barbecue sauce.

- Day 2: Culinary school. That's it. I'll be the best barbecue grill master. Or maybe I should apply for a Food Network show? If I hit it big, I can write a cookbook with the kids. And we can do our own video show.

- Day 3: A cookbook. A family barbecue cookbook. I like that. Or a podcast. How do you make money from a podcast?

- Day 4: I know. Family barbecues. I'll video them and put them on YouTube. And share recipes.

- Day 5: You know, I could maybe sell my special barbecue sauce. Make a website. Post family pics. And recipes. Maybe get advertisers.

- **Common Theme:** He wants to share his love of barbecue with his kids...and a yet-to-be determined audience on a yet-to-be determined platform...and find a way to make money from it.

If you feel like your life is off-kilter, your journal should help you pinpoint the primary cause or theme.

Work-Life Balance

Janie's work life is stable. A little boring, but low-stress. Janie lives with a roommate and commutes forty minutes each way (if she's lucky). She is in her late twenties and healthy, but she is not happy. She needs to make some changes, but where to start?

This is what she highlighted each day in her journal entries:

- Day 1: Work is boring. I wish they'd give me something challenging to do. Roommate had a fit over the way I loaded the dishwasher. OMG.

- Day 2: Feeling sluggish, maybe it was from eating fast food for three meals. Really did not want to deal with roommate from hell, so went to the bar after work.

- Day 3: Got a promo ad for the gym today. Should I do it? Roommate wants to be gym buddies. Blech. Maybe I can join a gym near work. Less rush-hour traffic and less roommate time.

- Day 4: I don't sleep well. Maybe I should eat better? Could be the noise from roomie fighting with her boyfriend.

- Day 5: Got a cool new project at work. Almost didn't mind the three-hour meeting. Hate when they schedule those for Friday. The weekend again. Great. Where can I go to hide from home?

- **Common Theme:** A new living situation with a shorter commute will lead to a happier and healthier lifestyle.

Take your answers and assign them a common two- to three-word theme.

Your theme will help you home in on what actions to take, interests to explore, or lifestyle elements to change as you get closer to identifying your specific destination.

Actions

- Career Change
- Climb Corporate Ladder
- Start Side Hustle
- Grow the Biz
- Become Screenwriter
- Produce Videos
- Develop Premiere Podcast

Interests

- Food
- Video
- Community Service
- Entrepreneurship
- Clothing Design
- Art
- Exercise

Lifestyle

- Healthy Life

- New Home

- Develop Passion

- Financial Independence

- Giving Back

- Continuing Education

- Relationship Development

In the next three chapters, we will transition your theme into a specific destination for your GoalTopia.

Chapter 8
Identify Options

Your theme will clue you into your GoalTopia location.

Part 1 of *Your Goal Guide* is very progressive. Each exercise builds upon the one before. Visualization leads you to your mission and motto. Through journaling, you will find your theme. Once you have your theme, you can home in on options for your ultimate goal and then decide which ones deserve further exploration.

The Glove Box

Your theme can lead you to a Pandora's Box of infinite possibilities. Each traveler is on his or her own journey. However, there are commonalities between people in similar situations.

Can you identify with any of the following?

GoalTopia is a Mountain Resort. A few years ago, out of necessity, Susan took a job she was overqualified for. She is content, but not overly enthused about the position or the industry and wants to see if there's something better out there. She would like to find a position more in line with her skills and experience that's in a different industry, so that's what she needs to look into.

GoalTopia is an Amusement Park. Kamila is a consultant who likes the flexibility of working from home. She needs to increase her income, but she'd rather not get a day job. The theme that came out of her journaling was to start an additional side hustle. She needs to identify her options for freelance businesses that would work alongside her consulting firm.

GoalTopia is the Big City. Carl lives in the Midwest and is about to retire. He had a long career as a teacher, yet always wanted to be an actor. Over the years, he performed in community theatre and even had bit parts in films that cast locals when they came to town. He was trying to identify his second act, something that made him happy and fulfilled, and all he could journal about was pursuing a career as a character actor (his theme). He needs to figure out if it's actually feasible and *which* big city to target. If Carl pursues theatre, it's the East Coast. If he pursues TV and film, he'll need to go out West. Or he can try a big city somewhere in between. Lots of options, much to research.

GoalTopia is the Beach. Alan works too much. He is either attached to his computer, producing events, or out networking. He gets up too early and works too late. His theme is that his life is out of whack. He must find ways to have better balance.

Options

In this chapter, you will choose ten options that embody your theme, and then narrow them down to three. As you identify what options are available to you, make sure they still align with your mission and motto, and propel you toward GoalTopia.

For instance:

GoalTopia: Happily employed
Mission: Quality work at a quality company
Theme: Appreciated at work
Options: Identify potential new jobs/career

GoalTopia: Successful business owner
Mission: Support other entrepreneurs
Theme: Offers products
Options: Identify what to create

GoalTopia: Respected expert
Mission: Share my passion
Theme: World-travel expertise
Options: Identify ways to become known for sharing knowledge on world travel

GoalTopia: Work-life balance
Mission: Enjoy the little things
Theme: Stop being a workaholic
Options: Identify potential lifestyle changes

What do you think you need to do to put your theme into action? What decisions do you need to make? Let's go back to planning.

Road Trip Exercise 8: Identify Options

Go to the next page in your dedicated notebook or document
and title it, "Options." Or use the worksheet in the back
of the book.

Based on your journal entries and notes, make a list of ten
possibilities of what you can do in service to your theme.

From that list, choose the five possibilities that hold the most
interest. *Note: You can always go back and explore more, but
this will get you started.*

Answer the following questions about your top five:

- Why does this interest me?

- How will it serve my mission and motto?

- In what ways is it a good fit for my theme?

- Which of my experience and skills can I use or transfer to
  pursue this?

- What additional education, support, and resources will I
  need to obtain?

From this information, you should be able to narrow your
options down to three finalists. These are the ones you will
research extensively.

Chapter 9
Research the Possibilities

Preparation leads to a successful journey.

You've decided about where you want to go on a road trip. You've narrowed locations down to three. So what's next? Before you make reservations, you want to make sure you choose the best place.

Whether you decide to go to the mountains, the amusement park, the city, or the beach, you want to check out the cost, distance, and amenities of the accommodations. You'll also need to look at the community—hangouts, offerings, and atmosphere—as well as see what towns you need to drive through to get there.

The same is true for your goal trip routes. You have honed your options. Now it's time to do a deep dive into the possibilities before you choose one.

Value of Research

When researching potential goal trips, you need to gather enough information to know what you might be getting into, but not so much you get information-overload. This can cause you to become overwhelmed and discouraged by the long road ahead of you. No one wants that.

By doing research upfront, you not only tap into what excites you, you will be better equipped to plot out your goals and have a successful trip. And luckily, there are resources everywhere, specific to your goal trip.

You can learn what you need to get started by reading books and articles, listening to podcasts, watching videos, joining online and real-life communities, and talking to friends, peers, and others.

Compile your favorite websites and rally your troops. That way, you can ask your trusted network about the information you seek.

Detour: LinkedIn

If you are not already on LinkedIn, what's stopping you?

If you haven't updated your profile or posted in a while, now's the perfect time to rejoin the platform.

LinkedIn is a business-focused social network, which means it can be the biggest asset for your professional goals. Use LinkedIn for researching potential jobs and industries as well as to connect with friends and peers. It may even help with your personal goals. LinkedIn is less cluttered than most other social networks, so you are more likely to see your connections and be seen.

Later, when we get into networking in Chapter 23, we'll go into using LinkedIn for developing relationships with new connections and increasing your visibility. But for now, let's make sure you are on the platform with a relatively up-to-date profile.

Go to LinkedIn.com. Sign in or create an account using your email address or Facebook account. LinkedIn has a user-friendly interface that will walk you through the process. *Note: There are paid LinkedIn account options, but you can skip them for now.*

Fill out your profile as accurately as possible, and make sure to include a recent picture for your profile, full contact information, and a brief and relevant intro. If you are concerned about an employer finding out that you are on LinkedIn, act like it's no big deal. You joined LinkedIn as an advocate for your company. They don't need to know you are being an advocate for yourself.

Connect with friends, peers, and former colleagues on the platform. The more robust your network, the more they will be able to help you and vice versa.

Road Trip Exercise 9A: Research

Go to the next page in your dedicated journal or document and title it, "Research." Or use the worksheet in the back of the book.

Take your top three options from the previous exercise and find out, specifically:

- What education is required?
- What resources exist?
- Who are the leaders in the field?
- What are the pros of entering the field?
- What are the cons?
- Do I want to pursue this path?

While a simple web search may get you started, you'll want to tap into your network to get more well-rounded information.

Road Trip Exercise 9B: Find Connections and Connectors

Go to the next page in your dedicated journal or document and title it, "Connections." Or use the worksheet in the back of the book.

First, think about all the companies and people you know personally who could give you more information about each option. Write them down.

Next, list the connectors in your network. It could be former colleagues, friends, or friends of friends. Add the people who seem to know everyone and if they don't, they know someone who knows someone, etc. Also, include people who do the sort of work you are exploring. The more individuals you list, the more likely you will find those who can help you.

Start by brainstorming a list of at least fifty people. These can be neighbors, your doctor, friends you met on vacation years ago, people from the coffee shop, your hairstylist. One idea will lead to so many others. Once you have your big list, narrow it to down to those who you think can best help you or know others who can.

For your top-tier people, gather the following:

- Name

- Email

- Phone number

- Website or LinkedIn profile

Leave space under their contact information for notes. Or start a new spreadsheet or Word document to track the information you gather.

Also designate which ones are *easy gets* versus those busy—but ideal—connections.

Begin with the easy gets, people who know and like you and will not hesitate to give you some time. This will give you confidence to keep moving forward. You can still reach out to those uber-busy ideal connections. Just be realistic with your expectations.

To your connectors. Jot a quick email or instant message asking if they have a few minutes to jump on the phone. Say that you know they are connected and are hoping they could direct you to those who know about *whatever* and provide an introduction.

To your relevant connections. Jot a quick email or instant message asking if they have a few minutes to jump on the phone or meet for lunch or coffee. You are looking into *whatever* and would appreciate some insight. Depending on the situation, you probably also want to ask that they keep your conversation between the two of you.

At the start of this exploration, you may not know what you don't know. That's okay. Conversations often lead to a bounty of information...and even more connections. Take lots of notes.

Remember to follow up with everyone. Send a thank you note, a real one, on paper that you put in the mail. That extra effort will show you really appreciate them sharing their time and knowledge with you.

Chapter 10
Select a Destination

*When you choose a destination that excites you,
you'll be even more motivated.*

Now that you have carefully researched what it takes to get to different places, you should have enough information to choose the location of your GoalTopia. Keep in mind this will likely be the first of many road trips in pursuit of your goals.

It's a matter of deciding where to go on *this* goal trip.

Destination Scenarios

For instance...

The Hopeful Employee. Ralph was laid off of his job last year, and the position he got a few months later didn't pan out either, to no fault of his own. He is increasingly disheartened by a revolving door of sending out résumés and interviewing for positions in his field with no success. Should Ralph keep trying? Or start from scratch in a new industry? And if he is going somewhere new, where would that be? That's what he needs to figure out.

The Consultant. Christina wants to expand her business, which means a trip on the roller coaster. But which amusement park? One option has her hiring more subcontractors so she can turn her small consulting business into an agency, while another would be to home in on a niche and grow her business that way. They are both viable. But what should she do?

The Expert. Rebecca wants to become known as an authority in the foodie space. That means she is headed for the "big city." But which one? Becoming an expert can present itself in different ways. She could be an author, an educator, or a voice through videos and podcasts. She needs to decide which of these versions is most aligned with who she is and her mission.

There is no one right destination, just as there is no one right path. There is just what's right for you right now.

One More Thing

While you want to make certain your path and destination align with your mission and theme, it doesn't need to be 100 percent on everything. If you are excited about the road you are about to take, 90 percent may be good enough. Ending up in GoalTopia—happily living your ideal life—is what matters.

Let's say you went into this process determined to get a full-time job while enjoying your side hustle as a fitness instructor. Your GoalTopia is to be happy, financially independent, and fully employed. In the research process, you figure out how to grow your side hustle into a fitness empire and decide you just need a part-time gig to tide you over. It's okay to go down that road.

Enthusiasm counts a lot as fuel. As long as you have the drive and you can see GoalTopia, it's okay to sway from the original road. That's what the discovery process is all about.

Road Trip Exercise 10: Destination Decision

Go to the next page in your dedicated notebook or document
and title it, "Destination Decision." Or use the worksheet in the
back of the book.

Review the previous sections for GoalTopia, Mission Statement,
Motto, and Theme.

Before you commit to a destination, for each of your top three
possibilities, ask yourself:

- Does this choice match my original vision?

- Is it aligned with my mission and motto?

- Does it support my theme?

- What, if any, adjustments will I need to make to my life
  to pursue this?

- Do I want to do this?

From your answers, you should be able to determine which
possibility best aligns with your definition of GoalTopia, your
mission, your motto, and your theme.

Okay, now you may choose.

Remember, this is written in ink, not stone. You can always go
back and explore other options. Just be sure to give it enough
time to make a concerted effort.

SECTION 3

Brainstorm Your Route: Your Path

You've selected a specific destination for GoalTopia. Awesome. Time to plan your road trip! Now, you get to decide where and when to drive as well as what day trips—a.k.a. short-term goals—to incorporate into your journey.

Depending on your specific destination, here's an idea of how this section may play out:

GoalTopia: Mountain Resort/Work Change

- Specific Destination: Establish successful new career in _____

- Long-Term Goal: Find a position in _____, working for a _____ company

- Short-Term Goals: Attain education and skills required for new career path

- Benchmarks: Enroll in continuing education

- Tasks: Research programs and internships, redo résumé

GoalTopia: Amusement Park/Successful Business Owner

- Specific Destination: Become the top company that does _____

- Long-Term Goal: Launch _____ business

- Short-Term Goals: Set up X, Y, Z, create promotions, get sales, and assemble team

- Benchmarks: Develop online presence, create business entity

- Tasks: Create logo, branding, marketing plan, and determine product or service

 ## GoalTopia: Big City/Known Expert

- Specific Destination: Become renowned and recognized author

- Long-Term Goal: Write bestselling books

- Short-Term Goals: Write book and book proposal, find agent

- Benchmarks: Marketing plan, social media strategy, start a blog

- Tasks: Create branding

Destination: Beach/Personal Goals

- Specific Destination: Happy life in a new home

- Long-Term Goal: Move to a new place

- Short-Term Goals: Schedule movers, switch utilities, donate what you no longer need, shop for new items

- Benchmarks: Schedule appointments, look at possible new homes

- Tasks: Research areas, sign up for listings, decide what you need/are willing to accept

In these five chapters, you will brainstorm all the goals, benchmarks, and action items you believe are necessary to get to your destination before putting together a plan—an itinerary—for your trip to GoalTopia.

Chapter 11
Brainstorm All Goals

Brainstorming and overthinking don't mix.

You've spent a lot of time and energy zeroing in on what you think would make you happy. I've mentioned before that planning is essential in figuring out what you want and how to get it. There's a fine balance between overthinking and underthinking. Brainstorming enables you to do a little bit of both.

Effective Brainstorming

You know how sometimes less is more? With brainstorming, more is more. You want to write down as many things as possible so you have more goals to sort and schedule.

When brainstorming any sort of list, keep in mind:

- The first five to ten items come tumbling out of your head
- The next five or so take more thought, but still come to you fairly easily
- Anything beyond that, you really have to stretch your brain

Sometimes you end up prioritizing the things at the start of your list. Other times, the last item is the most important.

The more you come up with, the more options you have to play with as you plan your trip to GoalTopia.

Road Trip Exercise 11: Goals Brainstorm

Go to the next page in your dedicated notebook or document and title it, "Goals Brainstorm." Or use the worksheet in the back of the book.

Write Down All of Your Goals

Many of these should be related to your GoalTopia. But you also should put in everything you want to accomplish:

- Short- and long-term goals
- Personal and professional goals
- Easy goals, realistic goals, and dream goals
- Simple action items and tasks
- Anything you want to do or have been meaning to do and haven't gotten around to doing

The reason to set both professional and personal goals is because they work in tandem. Organize your personal life and you set up your professional life for success. Be happy in your career and your quality of life will improve.

At this point, the order is unimportant. You'll organize it later. The key is to get your goals out of your head and put them onto a piece of paper where you can see them.

Write out twenty goals.

Now write fifty more.

On a roll? Make it an even one hundred.

Brainstorm Hack: Go Analog and then Digital

Your master list can be on paper, electronic, or both (*my preference*). Use a notepad or your journal to list out all of your long-term and short-term goals, benchmarks, and tasks. Then, type it up. You will come up with things you may have forgotten the first time around. Plus, a digital list is easier to divide and organize.

Keep previous variations of any lists. Just save them by adding the date to the title and print out the revision.

If you get stuck, or even after you finish your list, look at your visualization exercise, future bio, mission statement, journaling pages, or option worksheets to see if you missed anything.

Sample Goals

Here are fifty examples of goals that span different personal and professional GoalTopias; some even overlap. These are a combination of my clients' and my community's brainstorms as well as the Goal Survey. They are, intentionally, all over the place. Take or adapt what is applicable to get you started:

- Be 100 percent self-employed

- Earn five thousand dollars per month income from my business

- Make six-figures working part-time hours

- Create a workable budget

- Lose X pounds

- Do a better job of self-care

- Set up a home recording studio

- Continue to learn and innovate

- Be successful and have fun doing it

- Release my first album of songs

- Create financial freedom

- Explore career opportunities

- Set up business systems to be more efficient

- Find a hobby

- Write and sell a screenplay

- Perform at cafés regularly

- Obtain better organizational skills

- Write a book

- Start a podcast

- Attend twenty plus hours of professional development a month

- Read at least two books a month

- Join a gym

- Launch product

- Turn my hobby into a business

- Get more media to promote my business

- Sell lots of stuff on eBay

- Find an investor

- Make a living solely as an artist

- Create an app

- Secure full-time employment

- Redo my résumé

- Update my LinkedIn profile

- Quit my day job

- Be more active on social media

- Live more in the present

- Present at more conferences

- Generate solid friendships

- Resolve medical issues

- Build a treehouse

- Get out of a toxic relationship

- Spend more time with my family

- Improve my website

- Clean and organize my home

- Go on more dates

- Get married

- Have a baby

- Move

- Buy a house

- Travel

Chapter 12
Organize Professional Goals

To conquer, you must first divide.

Goals work together; they build upon each other. Long-term goals are comprised of short-term goals, short-term goals are made from benchmarks (milestones), and benchmarks are compiled from tasks (action items).

Let's break it down.

Long-Term Goals Are Comprised of Short-Term Goals

On your road trip you will make a variety of stops (short-term goals) on the way to your destination (long-term goal).

Before getting a million downloads on YouTube (long-term goal), you need to launch your video series, get a lot of subscribers, and create and execute a promotion plan (short-term goals).

Short-Term Goals Are Made from Benchmarks

Each time you stop at a different location (short-term goal), you will explore multiple places (benchmarks). If you stopped at Sedona during a drive to the Grand Canyon, you'd visit many local shops.

Before launching your video series (short-term goal), you will need to create your channel and produce videos. Those are benchmarks.

Benchmarks Are Compiled from Tasks

At each place (benchmark), you will do different things (tasks). At the make-your-own pottery shop, you create a mug, paint it, and then wait while it goes in the kiln.

In order to create your YouTube channel (benchmark), you need to decide on and design your branding, get social media identities, and sign up for an account. These are all tasks.

Tasks make up benchmarks. Benchmarks make up short-term goals. Short-term goals lead to long-term goals.

Separate Professional from Personal Goals

Before we address your long- and short-term goals, separate your master list into two categories: Professional Goals and Personal Goals. Group similar goals together. *We will address your personal goals in the next chapter.*

Electronically. Copy and paste your master list into a new professional goals document. Then cut and paste the personal goals into a separate document. Or print out your list.

On Paper. Take a highlighter and note which are the professional goals. Rewrite professional and personal goals onto separate lists.

Sample Professional Goals

These are the professional goals pulled from Chapter 11, grouped with other like items:

- Create financial freedom
- 100 percent self-employed
- Earn five thousand dollars per month income from my business
- Make six-figures working part-time hours
- Turn my hobby into a business
- Find an investor
- Launch product
- Create an app

- Improve my website
- Improve my craft
- Present at more conferences
- Start a podcast
- Get more media

- Explore career opportunities
- Redo my résumé
- Update my LinkedIn profile
- Secure full-time employment
- Quit my day job

- Set up a home recording studio
- Release my first album of songs
- Perform at cafés regularly
- Make a living solely as an artist
- Be more active on social media

- Continue to learn and innovate
- Attend twenty plus hours of professional development a month
- Be successful and have fun doing it
- Set up business systems to be more efficient
- Obtain better organizational skills

- Write and sell a screenplay
- Write a book

Road Trip Exercise 12: Professional Goals Map

Go to the next page in your dedicated notebook or document and title it, "Professional Goals Map." Or use the worksheet in the back of the book.

Take your list of professional goals and identify which are the long-term goals. Ideally, these all somehow relate to your mission and GoalTopia. Whether you are using your journal or a computer document, put a different long-term goal on top of each page. *Keep in mind that long-term goals can take one to five years or even a lifetime.*

Now, put any short-term goals from your list under the appropriate long-term goal. Leave space below each short-term goal. *Short-term goals can be accomplished in as little as one to six months.*

Now, add benchmarks under each short-term goal. These are mini-hurdles. For instance, if your long-term goal is to raise funds for and visibility of your philanthropy, a short-term goal might be to plan the annual event. Benchmarks might include figuring out the logistics (day, place, time), support (what needs to be outsourced), and features (emcee, silent auction, entertainment). Many of these benchmarks and tasks may already be on your master list, but you may think of things you need to add.

Under each benchmark, write out the tasks necessary to accomplish it. Again, some action items will come from your list, while others will occur to you during this process. For instance, a short-term term goal, such as launching a blog, will require benchmarks like creating branding, content strategy, and imagery. You also need to address the technical aspects, which is another benchmark. Deciding on hosting, the URL, and the template are all tasks you might need to add.

Are there any additional action items that didn't make their way onto your lists? Check your mission. Do any of those action items relate to your mission? Do they serve another purpose? If the answer is yes, add those items to the bottom of your list.

These can include:

- Extremely long-term reach or dream goals to keep on your radar
- Supplementary short-term projects
- Additional resources, education, and tools

You can add to these lists at any time.

Goal Map: Build a Biz Selling X

If building a successful business is your long-term goal, determine what smaller goals are involved in making it a reality.

Long-term goal: Build a successful business

Short-term goal: Launch a website

Benchmark: Design website

Tasks:

- Determine site map
- Figure out branding: select logo, colors, design template
- Write content: about page, products/services/locations, team, press (each page of content is a task)
- Hire an editor to proof it
- Take pictures or purchase images for the site

Benchmark: Blog regularly

Tasks:

- Create a list of blog topics
- Write posts for your blog
- Write guest posts
- Create and maintain social media profiles
- Add social buttons so people can share your articles

Long-Term Goal: Launch product

Short-Term Goal: Create product

Benchmark: Build prototype or demo

Tasks:

- Decide which product type (electronic, invention, service)

- See what resources, skills, or people you need to help you create it

- Research cost

- Analyze options

- Get funding

Goal Map: Become a Known Expert

There may be overlap between building a successful business and becoming well-known. This map focuses on the latter.

Long-term goal: Become a bestselling author

Short-term goal: Write book

Benchmark: Research book

Tasks:

- Create chapter outline

- Do any relevant interviews

- Transcribe interviews

- Gather resources: quotes, graphics, links

Benchmark: Write book

Tasks:

- Write each chapter

- First edit

- Second edit
- Third edit
- Outside edit
- Review book

Short-term goal: Sell book

Benchmark: Write book proposal

Tasks:

- Research subject matter, demographics, and competitors
- Elevate social media presence
- Draft components
- Write sample chapter
- Review and rewrite book proposal

Benchmark: Get an agent

Tasks:

- Research agents
- Go to author events and network
- Write and submit queries

Long-term goal: Become an in-demand keynote speaker

Short-term goal: Get speaking engagements

Benchmark: Build platform

Tasks:

- Update website, branding, and social media to reflect this objective

- Create videos so people who come to your website are able to observe your style

- Write a book

Benchmark: Research possibilities

Tasks:

- Ask friends/peers for recommendations

- Expand your network

- Target appropriate events and go to them

Benchmark: Speaking outreach

Tasks:

- Create a press kit and/or tab on your website

- Write a query letter

- Reach out to local groups and eventually national organizations

Goal Map: Fulfilling New Career

If you are pursuing an entirely different career rather than a position at a similar company, your route will be a bit different. However, some of the principles apply to both.

Long-term goal: Climb the corporate ladder

Short-term goal: Get hired

Benchmark: Decide what you want

Tasks:

- Write up your ideal situation

- Search for companies that fit
- Target positions you want

Benchmark: Revise your online persona to reflect
                ideal position

Tasks:

- Update résumé
- Write cover letter
- Revise LinkedIn, portfolio, and/or website

Benchmark: Outreach

Tasks:

- Check in with your peers and trusted connectors
- Go to events in your field
- Expand your network

Benchmark: Seek and apply for jobs

Tasks:

- Set up job alerts on LinkedIn and other sites
- Apply for jobs
- Request introductions through mutual connections
- Follow up
- Interview
- Get hired

Add this if you are seeking a career change.

Short-term goal: Choose career

Benchmark: Explore potential careers and requirements

Tasks:

- Learn more: search web, watch videos
- Find connections in the field and set up informational interviews
- Look into training and continuing education
- Educate yourself

Benchmark: Set up informational interviews

Tasks:

- Ask your key connectors for recommendations
- Make a list of people to approach
- Email potentials to request a time to speak
- Set a time to talk via phone, Skype, or in-person
- Prepare questions
- Conduct interviews; take notes either during or after
- Write thank you notes by hand and mail them

Chapter 13

Organize Personal Goals

Your personal goals deserve the same energy as your professional ones.

Personal goals complement professional ones. When you do things to improve your personal life, it impacts your career, and vice versa. Whether your personal goals are related to projects or lifestyle changes, they should be taken seriously. Getting to the decision to make a life-change is a big deal and should be treated as such.

Project Personal Goals

Some personal goals lend themselves to an organized pursuit. Think of this as a road trip that requires multiple scheduled stops, such as going to visit family in different parts of the country or dropping your kid off at college.

Project personal goals are structure-based, so you map them out and manage them the same way you navigate a professional goal. For instance, if your goal is to find a new place to live, complete a home-improvement project, or train for a competition, you would break it down into short-term goals, benchmarks, and tasks.

Lifestyle Personal Goals

On the other hand, more ongoing and less structured personal goals can be pursued in a more organic way and be accomplished simply by changing your routine. In road trip language, these could be more of a staycation—adventures you can have, things you can change without leaving your home—or day trips—short distance, low-commitment action items.

For instance, lifestyle personal goals can range from getting healthy and spending quality time with your family to reading regularly and expanding your network. For these types of goals, you would make an extensive list of action items related to the goal and then set aside time each day or each week to work on them.

Overlaps

Some personal goals start project-based and turn into lifestyle adjustments.

Finding a hobby is a project goal. You need to put a plan in place to discover your options, gather necessary tools/equipment, try them out, and decide on your favorite(s). Once you choose one and include it in your routine, it becomes a lifestyle goal.

Divide Personal Goals

Before we move on to the next exercise, take your list of personal goals and indicate which are project-based and which are lifestyle.

Project-Based Personal Goals

- Find a hobby
- Sell lots of stuff on eBay

- Resolve medical issues
- Build a treehouse
- Get out of a toxic relationship
- Clean and organize my home
- Get married
- Have a baby
- Move
- Buy a house

Lifestyle Personal Goals

- Create a workable budget
- Lose X pounds
- Do a better job of self-care
- Read at least two books a month
- Join a gym
- Live more in the present
- Generate solid friendships
- Spend more time with my family
- Go on more dates
- Travel

Road Trip Exercise 13A: Project Personal Goals

Go to the next page in your dedicated notebook or document and title it, "Personal Project Goals." Or use the worksheet in the back of the book.

Select your project-based long-term personal goals and map them out as you would your professional goals. If you are using your journal or a computer document, put a different personal goal on top of each page. *Keep in mind that since the stakes are different, long-term personal goals generally take less time than long-term professional goals.* Then, list out short-term goals, benchmarks, and tasks.

Just like with your professional goals, you may want to chart your goals on paper. Then type them up so you have a clean copy you can add to—and print out—at any time.

Goal Map: Home as a Gathering Place

Long-term goal: Make our house feel like a home

Short-term goal: Renovate the yard

Benchmark: Create outdoor dining area

Tasks:

- Research options
- Decide what you want
- Get quotes from contractors for upgraded patio
- Hire contractors
- Shop: decide what you like, compare prices, order
- Decorate
- Enjoy

Benchmark: Build a treehouse

Tasks:

- Research how to build a treehouse
- Decide on type of treehouse
- Get design
- Gather tools and supplies
- Build
- Decorate

Road Trip Exercise 13B: Lifestyle Personal Goals

Go to the next page in your dedicated notebook or document and title it, "Lifestyle Personal Goals." Or use the worksheet in the back of the book.

Take your lifestyle personal goals, group similar items together, and assign them a category name. For instance, anything health, eating, and fitness-related would be attributed to a healthy lifestyle. Put all relationship and family goals together, activity goals, etc. *Note: There may be some overlap.*

For example:

Healthy Living: Lose X pounds, do a better job of self-care, live more in the present, join a gym

Relationship & Family: Generate solid friendships, spend more time with my family, go on more dates

Activity: Read at least two books a month, join a gym, travel

Once you figure out your groupings, list the category on top of each page and add the sub-goals from your initial list. Now, do some brainstorming to fill out your pages. Think of this as turbo Directed Journaling.

Set a timer for fifteen minutes.

Ask and answer one question: what does (*this category*) mean to me? You want to think in terms of lifestyle changes: things you can do on a daily, weekly, and monthly basis that will add up and make a big difference.

Healthy Living. Come up with ways you can incorporate healthy eating, physical fitness, etc. into your life. It may mean exercising three times a week, eating out only once a month, going to the grocery story weekly, bringing lunch to work, etc.

Relationship & Family. Are you angling to repair a relationship, find a new one, or get rid of a toxic one? What sorts of actions would "improve" your family situation? This might mean no cellphones at dinner, a family outing once a week or once a month, or one-on-one time with each kid.

Activity. The activity category can simply be a long list of places to go and things to do. It can range from networking activities and intramural sports to favorite resources to find and locations of activities.

Have at it.

When the timer goes off, you can stop. But if you are on a roll, keep going.

Lifestyle Brainstorm Hack: Expand Your Categories

Start a bonus page with new categories to add. During the brainstorm, new things will occur to you. That's the nature and purpose of such an activity. For instance, you wrote down bringing lunch as a Healthy Living goal, and you made the connection that it would also be good for Saving Money. Why not explore other Saving Money goals, too? Add it to your adjunct list and brainstorm more later.

Once you have a living, breathing list of how to reach personal lifestyle goals, figure out how to fit the related action items into your life. This includes what sort of time-commitment you can make, as well as what logistics are involved.

Friendship Goals

If your goal is to develop solid friendships, make a list of activities you enjoy (classes, trade shows, sporting events) and places to go (a favorite coffee shop, a walk around your neighborhood, a gallery opening) to shake things up. When you put yourself out there, you never know who you will meet. Put it in your schedule to try out something new each month.

Family Goals

If your goal is to spend more time with your family, make an appointment for everyone to get together at least once a week. As a family, come up with a list of things you'd like to do. Then, when you get together, pick that day's activity from a hat.

Money Goals

After you come up with the money-saving list, try a different thing each week or every other week. Keep the items that make a difference and replace the ones that do not. A lot of this process is trial and error. The more you try, the more you will be able to figure out.

Anything Else?

Are there any additional action items that didn't make their way on to your lists? These can include:

- Extremely long-term reach or dream goals to keep on your radar

- Supplementary personal project goals

- Additional lifestyle personal goals

You can add to your lists at any time.

Chapter 14
Prioritize

Beware of goal overload!

I know what you're thinking, "That's a lot of goals!" And that may be true. But the more goals, benchmarks, and action items you have, the easier it is to narrow them down and prioritize. It's kind of like how you can't edit anything unless you write it first. Or you can't make a sandwich until you know what's in the refrigerator. You can't make an informed decision unless you have all the information.

For instance:

GoalTopia is a Mountain Resort. While a job change is inevitable, you can now look at it with hope for something better, rather than fear. So, do you stick with the old job and pursue a lateral move, get the education you need to start on a different path, or find a solution that is a little of both?

GoalTopia is an Amusement Park. You have been riding the small-business roller coaster for way too long, and it feels like you are going in circles. You are. It's time to level-up. But is the solution new products, new services, or additional staff? Which gets the priority?

GoalTopia is the Big City. You want to see your name in lights, so people can learn from your knowledge and experience. You narrowed your long-term goals down to three: write a bestseller, launch a successful podcast, become a sought-after keynote speaker. Which avenue will you pursue first?

GoalTopia is the Beach. You have spent a lot of time building up your business, and it's time to put family first. But what does that mean? You can find a common interest and start a side hustle with your kids, embark on a family home project, or start a series of family adventures. Which can you best fit into your life while bringing you closer to the goal of balance?

Assigning Priority

Prioritizing is simple. When trying to decide what takes priority, ask yourself:

Is it exciting? Am I enthusiastic enough about the destination that the excitement and adrenaline will keep me going, even when the rest of life seems to have gotten the better of me?

Is it necessary? What are the prerequisites? Does one goal need to come before any others due to education, research, or timing?

Is it urgent? Are you unemployed and need a job? Do you need to leave work due to a toxic situation? Do you need to make a plan for something time-sensitive at home?

If, at any point, you are stumped by any decisions, go back to your idea of GoalTopia. Which goals do you need to embrace first and foremost to lead you to that perfect life?

Road Trip Exercise 14: Priorities

Go to the next page in your dedicated notebook or document and title it, "Priorities." Or use the worksheet in the back of the book.

From your extensive list, choose three of the long-term goals that will lead you to GoalTopia. One of these may be a dream goal, but the other two can be more realistic. *Remember, long-term goals can take one to five years.*

Next, choose three long-term personal goals. These act as support and should work in concert with your professional goals.

Now zero in. Choose three short-term professional and three short-term personal goals. These are the goals you will pursue in order to make those long-term goals happen. *Short-term goals can take one to six months, though sometimes longer.*

At the bottom of the page, write down the long-term and short-term goals you plan to address next. That way, once you achieve some of your short-term and long-term goals, you know what's coming up in your pipeline. Plus, you can do some minimal prep in your downtime. And, you'll be ready to go when the timing is right.

Priority Goals: Entrepreneur

- Three Long-Term Professional Goals
  - Get on *Forbes*'s 50 Under 50 List
  - Have my product placed on a TV show
  - Appear on a talk show

- Three Short-Term Professional Goals
  - Create and execute new social media marketing plan
  - Create a hot new product
  - Develop public speaking skills

- Three Long-Term Personal Goals
  - Lose X pounds
  - Grow my network
  - Save money for retirement

- Three Short-Term Personal Goals
  - Grocery shopping weekly, eat out twice a month
  - Networking events three times a month
  - Put $X aside each month

- On-Deck Long-Term Goals
  - Buy a house
  - Travel the world
  - Write a book

- On-Deck Short-Term Goals
  - Redecorate
  - Learn a new skill
  - Get my passport

Chapter 15
Choose Alpha and Beta Projects

As much as you may try, you can't do everything.

You have now amassed a variety of long- and short-term personal and professional goals that you will need to achieve on your road to GoalTopia. Even though you prioritized, you can't possibly pursue them all simultaneously. This is especially true if you, like most people, already have a slew of other obligations. You know: day job, social life, family. However, what you *can* do is choose alpha and beta projects.

It's just like it sounds. Choose one primary and one secondary project to work on in tandem with whatever else you have going on in your life. Feel free to mix and match your professional and personal goals.

Alphas and Betas

Like freeways and back roads, alpha and beta projects work together...and usually tag team. Sometimes, you need to slow down and take the scenic route. Other times, you just need to rev the engine and get on the freeway.

This is how and why you need alpha and beta projects.

You Don't Get Stalled

It's a Hollywood stereotype. Someone asks pretty much anyone in the business, "What are you working on?" And the standard answer is, "I have various projects at multiple stages of development." Now, that may be seen as code for, "Bartending while waiting for my next big gig," and it could be. But you will not get anywhere by standing in one place. When you take that statement literally and have more than one project in motion, it keeps the progression going. If you get stalled or need a break from your main project, you have another one prepped and waiting in the wings.

For example, Kevin is a corporate writer and musician. His primary goal is to build his business, but he also wants to build his audience and perform around town. His GoalTopia is not having to look for work; clients come to him so he can pick and choose the projects he wants. That gives him plenty of time to practice, write songs, and seek out gigs.

Each week, Kevin schedules his client work as well as time for practicing. Since Kevin's alpha (primary) project is developing an ongoing client base, he has a list of action items in pursuit of that goal. When he needs to switch gears, he has his beta (secondary) project of finding and submitting to musician showcases, as well as performing and posting on social media. This keeps him excited and moving forward on one or the other at all times.

Certain beta projects are imperative for anyone with a business, whether it's product or service, online or brick-and-mortar. Ongoing beta projects include:

- Updating your website

- Building your social media presence

- Taking photos or videos of your location, product, or service

Beta projects for those in the midst of changing their job or career may include:

- Searching job sites
- Writing targeted versions of your résumé
- Going to or volunteering at events

The key with the tandem alpha and beta is variety. If one project is dull, but necessary, make certain the other reminds you about why this trip is exciting in the first place.

Some Projects Are Meant to Be Together

While it doesn't always happen, sometimes your projects will complement each other. Batching similar tasks may propel your alpha and beta projects forward simultaneously. Other times, you'll find a more natural, mutually beneficial progression.

For instance, if you are producing (alpha) and promoting (beta) a podcast—or any content—certain items can be done at the same time.

- Your episode cover image can easily be reformatted for all of the major social media platforms
- Your episode description can be shortened and modified for use on Twitter, Facebook, and Instagram

This process also applies to writing a business website and creating a press kit; writing a book and a complimentary book proposal; and starting a non-profit and working through the 501(c) paperwork and grant requests. Some of the content will overlap.

In addition, certain personal and professional projects may be mutually beneficial:

- You want to improve your health and grow your network. Joining a gym could accomplish both.

- You want to date more and learn to cook; find a cooking class for singles.

- You want to be more social, be healthy, and save money. Start a weekly walking club.

You get the idea. So what will you take on first...and second?

Road Trip Exercise 15: Alpha and Beta Goals

Go to the next page in your dedicated notebook or document and title it, "Alpha Project." Title the page after that, "Beta Project." Or use the worksheet in the back of the book.

Referring to the previous page, what long-term goal will you address first?

Which alpha project will take center stage?

A good alpha project:

- Is timely

- Is important

- Makes you feel like you are making strides toward GoalTopia

Now choose a beta. Remember, the beta can be a short-term goal that relates to this or a different long-term goal.

A good beta project:

- Is less time-bound

- Is integral

- Makes you feel like you are taking steps toward GoalTopia

You may want to choose a beta that relates to a personal goal so you have that balance between personal and professional activity.

Next, list out the benchmarks and tasks for your alpha and beta projects.

Note any overlaps or symmetry.

Got them? Great.

Congratulations. You've chosen your route. After a little goal trip prep in the next section, you'll be on your way.

PART 2
Rules of the Road

You have goals. You have a plan. You have committed to make a change. This is all very exciting. But how do you get to your destination when there are bound to be challenges along the way?

- **Be Prepared.** Know what you are going to do, when you will do it, and why. Those are the building blocks for a successful journey.

- **Be Flexible.** As much as you prepare, things will not always go smoothly. Whether it's a flat tire or a flaky resource, something will happen that requires you to take a break, breathe, and reconfigure the GPS.

- **Be Healthy.** Taking care of yourself is a huge part of going through a transition successfully. Change—whether it's a job, a home, a relationship—is stressful. So do what you need to do to approach this trip from as healthful a place as possible. It will serve you well for the smooth roads as well as the bumpy ones.

Preparation, flexibility, and health go hand-in-hand. Part 2 of *Your Goal Guide* has everything you need for a fun and productive journey. First, we'll go through Tips for a Successful Trip. This includes advice for focus, time management, and balance. In the next section, we will deal with Car Maintenance and Troubleshooting. It includes ways to set yourself up for success as well as tips for dealing with those pesky detours.

In college, I competed on the speech team. This was individual events, not debate; I would write and deliver speeches as well as participate in the limited prep and dramatic readings categories. *Note: Speech, whether it's taking classes in school or joining a group like Toastmasters as an adult, is invaluable for developing your communication skills. If you're looking for one thing to improve your professional skillset, public speaking gets my highest recommendation.*

Whereas my trek across country was my most significant road trip, my time in college afforded me a variety of mini-journeys during competition season. Every weekend, my teammates and I would go to a new and exciting location...okay well, maybe the classrooms at random colleges in the Midwest were not *that* exciting, but the principles of prep, flexibility, and health all applied.

We spent hours every week prepping for the next competition. We used our skills and education (there were some journalism and communication students, but also political science, education, pre-law, and pre-med) and background (some of us were from small towns, others big cities) to write, practice, and prepare. Then, usually super-early on Saturday morning, we would drag ourselves to the university van armed with our speeches and other materials, overnight bags, and snacks. (Snacks, again. I know. Priorities.) The ride to the competition was all about the prep; we would be focused, practiced, in the zone.

Once at our destination, anything could happen. Usually it was business as usual. You perform, get your score, and see if you move on to the next round. Low attendance in a category could mean that room locations had changed, and we'd find ourselves dashing across campus to the next event. We could thrive, we could get the hiccups, and we might have an incident with a leaky Jelly doughnut moments before going on stage. We could give the best speech of our lives, and there would be someone better.

We learned to expect the unexpected, keep smiling (at least in public), and roll with it. We'd remain professional and know that if things didn't go our way, we could course-correct and try again. If we were eliminated, we'd go to the final rounds of our teammates and cheer them on. We watched out for each other, "Did you eat today? Here's a granola bar." "Oh, did you see X? Yeah, you were better. Maybe next week the judges will see that too."

Rides home were about recovering: bonding, talking, and supporting each other. On the longer trips, we would stop at a park, a chain restaurant, or lookout point for what our advisor called "mandatory fun." We made the trip part of the adventure. And at the end of the journey, we were ready for the next week of "prep, perform, thrive." It's not about avoiding the bumps, it's about paving over them and finding a better way to do it with the support of those around you.

SECTION 4

Tips for a Successful Trip

Whether working on a project or planning a road trip, you want the pavement to be as smooth as possible. Chapters 16 through 20 contain simple tricks and tips for time management and productivity.

Before you hit the open road, here are few things you can do to prep for your journey.

Clean Your Car/Find a Suitable Workspace

Whether or not your goals are directly related to what you are doing right now, make space to work on them.

- **Office Space.** A physical space will help you concentrate as well as validate the importance of your project.

- **A Drawer.** If a full physical space is not an option, then assign a drawer or cabinet in your home.

- **A File Box.** If you are working on the go—using your lunch breaks for your side hustle or to find another job—get one of the portable file boxes from your local office supply and set up shop in your car.

Regardless of your physical workspace, keep a folder on your computer hard drive or the digital cloud with electronic files from your work-in-progress and have a back-up system in place.

When you keep all of your materials together, especially when time is limited, you can jump into your goals whenever, and wherever, it is feasible.

Empty Your Trunk/Clear the Decks

Before you start anything new, take some time to get rid of any excess baggage. This can mean tying up loose ends, putting away a stalled project, or doing a purge of the aforementioned office to make room for exciting things ahead.

Bonus points for an electronic cleanse. Archive old files. Then, go through your inbox, read and respond to any lingering emails, and unsubscribe to any email lists that are no longer relevant. Consider using an email sorting program for that last task. This will save you a ton of time...time that can be better spent elsewhere.

One more thing. Be sure to clear mental space. If you recently got over a breakup, recovered from illness, or dealt with spill-over chaos (a.k.a especially draining family or friend drama), it may not be the best time to embark on something that needs your full focus. You should never drive when you are exhausted, right? If this is the case, take a little extra time planning so you are better able to take on new responsibilities.

Fill the Tank/Gather Resources

Go back to your notes from your research phase and identify any resources you may need to move forward toward your goals.

- **Office.** Do you need new notebooks? Other office supplies? How about a frame for your visualization exercise? Gather the things that you need to make your office not only inviting, but user-friendly.

- **Education.** Make a list of courses, books, podcasts, websites, etc. that will help you achieve your goals. *Your Goal Guide* is a roadmap, but you will need other resources to get you out of the starting gate. Some you may want to purchase now and others can wait. An ongoing list of what you need will help you identify items as you need them.

- **Miscellaneous.** Coffee, snacks, work clothes (to dress for the job you want), workout clothes—whatever you need to get into and stay in the zone.

- **Also.** Get new business cards. You want to make sure people remember you—and what you do—and are able to contact you. Even if you already have a business card from work, you may want something that reflects your new path.

The *key* to setting yourself up for success before heading out on any adventure is to clear the decks and put as many things in place as feasible. That being said, there is such a thing as being too prepared. Some might call it procrastination. Others might say it is the desire for perfection. I think it's probably a mix.

One of my favorite phrases is, "Done is better than perfect." Sometimes, especially when you are just getting started, it's best to hit the road. And know that if you forgot to pack something, like toothpaste, you can always pick some up in the next town.

Now are you ready? Great. Time for next steps.

Chapter 16
Read the Signs

You can't achieve your goals unless you know
what they are.

This tip is simple: Post your goals everywhere...and remember
to look at them. You wouldn't take a road trip without looking
at the map, would you? Come on. Even after you set the GPS,
you are still going to look, right? It's the same thing with goals.

A while back, a friend told me that she writes down her goals at
the beginning of the year and then sticks them in a drawer. At
the end of the year, she looks at her list and then is pleasantly
surprised if she accomplished anything. While that may work
for some people, that's not how goals work for most. After I
picked up my jaw off the floor, I suggested she might have
better luck accomplishing her goals if she looked at them
regularly. She was willing to try it. And wouldn't you know, she
actually did...and her success level improved dramatically.

A continual reminder of your goals will work wonders in
helping you achieve them.

Road Trip Exercise 16: Goal Posting

If you haven't already done so, take your priority goals from
Chapter 14 and your alpha and beta project lists from Chapter
15, and add them to your Trip Map—that's the central location
in your office where you keep all of your visual cues—right
along with your mission statement, motto, and visual cues.

Also, write a Top Ten list of the goals you want to achieve in the next year. This is the list you will put in all the places you look at frequently.

For instance:

- Your office. *On your Trip Map.*

- Your kitchen. *There's room on the fridge, right?*

- On your computer. *Put it on your desktop wallpaper so you see the list every time you log on.*

- On your smartphone and/or tablet. *Goal lists make a great background pic.*

Up against a deadline? You may want to post your more urgent goals on sticky notes throughout your home.

Oil Change/Goal Review Schedule

Review and revise your Goal List regularly so you stay on track. However, you do not want to alter the big list so often that you question your progress.

Here's a handy rule of thumb:

- **Look at your list:** As much as possible
- **Read your list:** At least once a day
- **Review your list:** Once a week
  - Take a few minutes to note your progress

- **Update your list:** Once a month
  - Archive completed short-term goals and add new ones

- **Revise your list:** Once a quarter
  - Take an inventory of "distance traveled" see what needs to be added, altered, and archived

- **Start a new list:**
  - Today
  - The beginning of the year
  - When you are at a crossroads
  - When you need to make an important personal decision or otherwise alter your personal situation
  - When you are undergoing a professional transition

When you look at your goals with frequency, they stay on the top of your mind...and you are much more likely to accomplish them.

Chapter 17
Create Itineraries

To-do lists are your friends.

When planning a road trip, you make a list of everything you want to see along the way, don't you? It builds excitement. Plus, when you write things down beforehand, you don't miss anything.

It's the same concept with to-do lists. To-do lists—a.k.a. itineraries, a.k.a. tasks, a.k.a. action items—are a simple and effective way to stay organized and be more productive. When you write down the things you need to do and keep them in a central location, you don't need to spend brain power thinking about them. It's a huge time-saver.

Has this ever happened to you? You wake up in the middle of the night with a fantastic idea. It's absolutely brilliant. But you are too tired to get out of bed and search for paper and a pen. But that's okay, because it's such an amazing idea, you know you will remember it. And what happens in the morning? It is gone from your head, possibly forever.

Write. Everything. Down.

To-Do Lists

Wondering what to put on your lists? Anything and everything that has to do with your current responsibilities and your goal projects. This includes meetings, assignments, and deadlines as well as professional action items and personal errands.

As a solopreneur, I divide my list by client tasks, appointments, assignments, and personal projects. I also incorporate planned weekly blog posts, social media updates, website changes, outreach tasks (pitches, relationship development, and follow-up), and upcoming events.

Types of To-Do Lists

There are a few different options of places to keep your list, but it really boils down to analog, digital, or both.

Paper Lists. Keep a dedicated notebook only for your to-do's. At the start of every week, put the date on the top of the page and write your to-do's underneath. Then, as each day passes, add any other items that come up. Also, check things off as you do them. Remember, if you do something that's not already on the list, feel free to add it and then check it off so you get that burst of satisfaction. The reason I say check things off rather than cross them out is that way, you can track your activities throughout the week. *More on tracking in Chapter 19.*

Digital Lists. This is the same concept as the paper lists, just using a dedicated document, spreadsheet, or online cloud solution rather than a central notebook. Spreadsheets are not just for numbers. You can organize tabs for different projects or clients and use columns to differentiate the steps and note deadlines.

Another way to keep a digital list is as a calendar appointment. This is the type of list I use; I really like the simplicity.

Every Sunday, I set an appointment in my Google Calendar with my to-dos for the week. I keep a section for each client, one for each of my current projects, and a place for ongoing tasks. Throughout the week, as I set appointments or get new assignments, I add each to the appropriate list.

Here's the trick with digital calendars: Instead of deleting completed tasks, I write DONE in all caps after each accomplishment. At the end of the week, I copy the list and paste it into next week's appointment. Then I delete the DONEs and add any new items for the week.

Online Task Management Tool and/or App. I'd be remiss if I didn't mention the plethora of online list solutions. Download a simple notepad app or go with OneNote or Evernote, which has more features. If you want to use some form of project management software, Trello (Trello.com) is the most user-friendly. It's a visual tool where you can use boards, cards, and lists to organize your projects. They offer a free version, but you can upgrade for more space, options, and features.

Both. Like with your goal brainstorms, my recommendation is to start with a handwritten list and then transfer items to your digital repository. You can also do this the other way around. The reason this system is so effective is because as you rewrite your list, you will inevitably come up with items you missed. This is also the reason why I like to do rough drafts on paper whenever I start any new project.

Road Trip Exercise 17: To-Do Lists

Choose your list type.

Every Sunday night or Monday morning, write out your tasks for the week.

Divide them by client and/or project and add a miscellaneous section for personal tasks. The list can be as long or as short as you'd like. Include action items, tasks, calls, meetings, errands, etc. Put stars next to urgent items.

Throughout the week, add any new tasks to your list.

Check off (for paper) or write DONE next to tasks as you complete them.

At the end of the week, copy over any incomplete or ongoing tasks and add anything new.

To-do lists are great, but there's an essential trick to them. Lists are only effective if you remember to read them.

Chapter 18
Don't Drive Every Day

Breaks are an essential part of any journey.

Being on the road constantly is a surefire way to get burned-out quickly. Even commercial drivers must adhere to certain regulations.

Over the course of your road trip, take breaks, see the sights, and under no condition should you drive when you are exhausted. There are many tourist attractions on the road to GoalTopia. Some may relate to your ultimate goal, while others may be just for fun. The point is, you have enough going on in your journey. Pace yourself.

While the idea of working toward your goals every day is good in theory, it's not always realistic since you have plenty of other professional and personal responsibilities.

You are taking this trip to GoalTopia because you will eventually benefit from it. However, long-term goals take time. That's why I emphasize the value of visual cues to help you stay focused and motivated.

GoalTopia is a Mountain Resort. Embarking on a new job or career path is a means to an end, but an adventure, nonetheless. You are reconnecting with former colleagues, learning more about different industries, and applying for jobs in your quest for a better position.

GoalTopia is an Amusement Park. As the analogy implies, starting or growing your business means lots of ups and downs. You are developing a passion project or side business to increase your income, slowly and steadily.

GoalTopia is the Big City. Showcasing your expertise may mean writing a book or blog, hosting a podcast, or speaking publicly. Elevating your status in your field over time will bring you more visibility which should lead to more clients, customers, and/or fans.

GoalTopia is the Beach. Work-life balance doesn't happen immediately. Like any relationship, whether it's with yourself or others, you need to want it...and work for it!

All of the above could bring long-benefits benefits and, in many cases, financial rewards. But some weeks, you simply don't have enough time to dedicate to all of your goals. This is totally fine!

The 5 of 7 Rule

My 5 of 7 Rule serves to help you take the pressure off yourself as you work toward your goals while continuing to juggle everything else going on in your life. As a result, you will be less stressed and more productive.

The 5 of 7 Rule is exactly how it sounds:

- Work toward your GoalTopia five out of every seven days each week.

- This enables you to keep your objective top of mind while giving you ample downtime.

- It eliminates the fluster you feel when life happens and you need to skip a day or two.

Let's say you're going to work fifteen minutes a day on your project, which is a reasonable amount of time. If you miss a day, you decide to do thirty minutes the next day. You miss that one too, and you're up to forty-five. Well, if you can't manage fifteen minutes, you'll really have challenges finding thirty or forty-five. My point is this: if you miss a day, just skip it and do fifteen minutes the following day.

Don't get me wrong. If working toward your goals every day is feasible, go right ahead. However, when you really need it, allow yourself a day or two off, guilt-free.

Road Trip Exercise 18: 5 of 7 Rule

Look at your schedule.

Decide how much time is realistic to dedicate.

See what time of day is feasible and look for pockets of time.

5 of 7 Hack: Your Lunch

Lunchtime is the perfect opportunity to put in your 5 of 7. There is plenty you can do to bring you closer to achieving your goals.

- **GoalTopia Planning.** Whether or not you are able to actively work on your alpha or beta from the office—although, depending on your office situation, maybe you can—there's always one thing you can do: think. Thinking counts. But if you do that every day instead of actually working toward GoalTopia, that's cheating. You can use lunchtime to brainstorm new ideas, update your to-do lists, or write or draft website copy, blog posts, social media posts, queries, or other documents.

- **Set up a Lunch Meeting.** Plan a weekly lunch out that can be social or business-related, or alternate between the two. Use this time for a face-to-face meeting with industry peers, an informational meeting for exploratory purposes, or a long overdue catch-up with a former colleague. Networking, which I've mentioned before and will mention again in Chapter 23, is a huge part of making progress.

- **Run an Errand.** This may not seem directly related, but it will also help you on your trip. If you step away from the computer screen and run a quick errand, that's one less thing you have to do after work. Go to the grocery and get your non-perishables, run to the office supply store, pick up the gift you need for that party this weekend. As a bonus, you may even enjoy a bit of sunshine that is not obstructed by the office window. That is always a good thing.

- **Plan a Day Trip.** This can mean planning next steps for a benchmark on your goal trip or researching an actual day trip. Find a conference to attend, look into travel as part of a personal goal, or research somewhere fun to go to celebrate reaching a milestone.

- **Exercise.** If getting healthy is part of the Goal Plan, then make strides toward it during lunch. The obvious option is to go to the gym. However, especially if you live in a nice climate, you can also get in some steps by taking a brisk walk—or even a leisurely one—outside to break up your day. Weather not so good? There's always the mall.

- **Learn.** Is continuing education part of the plan? Watch a video, read a book, peruse websites. Do something that makes you more knowledgeable about what you want and where you are going.

- **Take a Break.** You work hard, and that means it's completely acceptable to do nothing every once in a while. Meditate, listen to music, read a book for fun, take a nap in your car, or watch something on Netflix. Just enjoy your "me" time. You will be more refreshed and ready to take on the rest of your day...and the rest of your goals.

It's not realistic to assume you can take a full non-working lunch every day of the week, especially if you work for someone else full-time. Yet if you set aside one or two days a week to do something different, you may find that shaking up your schedule makes you healthier, happier, and more productive.

When you decide ahead of time not to work on your project every day, it eliminates some of the pressure. Less pressure means clearer thinking. Clearer thinking means more progress. Little bits of time add up.

Chapter 19
Keep a Trip Log

Capture your journey, so you can revisit the sites.

Did you go on trips with your family when you were a kid? You'd take your 35mm camera—remember how cameras used to have film?—and snap pics of the things you saw during your travels. These days, who needs a camera when you have things like a cellphone that take even better pics? Open Instagram, add a filter, and make your photos look even better.

There have always been countless ways to capture an adventure. Maybe you'd write letters to friends back home. And perhaps you'd even start a journal. Sometimes you'd get a souvenir as a reminder of each location. As a child, I collected bells from every state I visited with my family. (Still have them, by the way.) When I drove to California, I picked up a few tourist flyers from the hotel in each city. These, along with a stack of paper maps with dog-eared pages and highlighted roads, are my great treasures from my journey. Plus my memories, of course.

Having a roadmap will guide you toward GoalTopia. However, you also need to gauge your progress, document the process, and enjoy the sites.

Calendaring

Throughout the course of your goal trip, schedule all of your time. Track what you cannot schedule and capture your milestones. This will keep your goals in forward motion while helping you stay motivated.

Scheduling. It's easy to get distracted from the task at hand. You have assignments and deadlines, emails and marketing, clients and meetings, and any number of unexpected things that come up on any given day. One long phone call or a late meeting can throw everything off. Add your alpha and beta goal projects into your normal workflow. There is only one way to make any progress. Divide out your action items and schedule them on your calendar. That way, you know what to do and when.

Goal Time. Set aside at least one or two hours each week—in fifteen, thirty, or sixty minute increments—to put toward your goals. This is especially important when you are using goals to pursue one thing career-wise, while working somewhere else. It's easy to get mired in have-to's and forget about the want-to's.

Personal Goals. Lifestyle goals work a little differently, since they are either changing a habit or redistributing downtime. When this is the case, it's more likely that you will designate a certain amount of time toward these goals each day, week, or month.

- For more relationship maintenance, you might schedule a date night once a week and a no-phones adventure on the first Saturday of the month.

- For healthy eating, schedule a trip to the grocery store every Saturday morning. Batch cooking-for-the-week responsibilities on Sunday nights.

- For saving money *and* family bonding, make a list of free or inexpensive local activities, put each one on a small sheet of paper, fold them, and then put them in a jar. Every Friday night at dinner, pick one to do the next day as a family.

Road Trip Exercise 19: Calendaring

Schedule all of your action items, not just ones that move you toward GoalTopia. The more organized you are, the more likely you will stay on track with *everything*.

Set up a recurring fifteen-minute appointment with yourself every Monday. Yes, I am suggesting you make an appointment to make appointments.

During this time:

- Schedule and/or confirm any meetings and events

- Slot in appointments for all of your primary action items. Work off the to-do list you made Sunday night/Monday morning. This includes client work, proposals, content creation, reporting, billing, etc. Depending on how you work best, schedule these in one- to two-hour increments

- Be sure to include goal time

- Add an optional appointment at the end of your week to tie up any loose ends

Also, make fifteen-minute appointments throughout the week for email, phone calls, and, if it's part of your workflow, social media marketing.

- **Email.** Set three fifteen-minute appointments each day: first thing in the morning, at lunchtime, and at the end of the day. Responding to each email as they come in distracts you from the projects at hand. Of course, some things are urgent, so deal with those in real-time. However, most emails can be sent in a batch at the time set aside for them.

- **Phone calls.** If phone communication is an essential part of your daily work, then treat it as a long appointment. However, if you are like me and the only time you talk on the phone (other than for meetings) is to make a hair appointment, call the mechanic, or book a lunch, one fifteen-minute slot for miscellaneous calls late in the day should be fine.

- **Social Media.** Those who have their own business or work in marketing know how important it is to maintain a social media presence. However, they also know how time-consuming it can be. Unless you work in social media or are participating in a Twitter chat, Facebook Live, webinar, or other online event, set aside two fifteen-minute social media increments (early and late in the day). Use your time to post, scan your feed, share (or retweet) others' articles, comment, and more.

Appointment Hack: The Timer

My favorite productivity tool is a timer. You can get a lot done in focused blocks of time. That means no email, no distractions, nada. Here are five ways to use a timer to increase your productivity.

Block Time. Set a timer when working during your scheduled time blocks so there's no need to keep an eye on the clock. Concentrate fully on your work. Then, when your timer goes off, finish what you're doing and move on to the next thing.

Avoid Social Media Tangents. Let's face it, although important for marketing your business, social media tends to be a time-suck. You log on in the morning to do a couple of things, you get distracted, and the next thing you know, it's almost noon. Set a timer for your fifteen-minute social media appointments so you receive a reminder to not fall into the social media abyss.

Limit Time-Consuming Tasks. This social media trick works well for emails and phone calls. Set a specific amount of time to assign boundaries to things that could otherwise spiral out of control. When the timer goes off, it's time to wrap it up and move on.

Take a Break. It's important to take breaks throughout the day, whether it's to stretch, get a bite to eat, or have a water-cooler or online conversation. However, if you spend your downtime checking your watch or the clock on your smartphone to see how much time you have left, are you actually disengaging? Put your phone in your pocket and be fully present.

Force Inspiration. Every now and then, you encounter a project that you can't quite get into. So instead of spending a bit of time to get it started, you avoid it. Hello, procrastination! This results in stress, not to mention a potential failed project. Set a timer for fifteen minutes and force yourself to concentrate on what is perplexing you. Then, when the timer goes off, if you've figured it out, keep going. If not, take a breath, move onto something else, and try again the following day. At least the project will be in your head, which will make it easier to tackle the next time.

While you can get an old-fashioned egg timer for any of these tasks, the timer on your smartphone is probably the easiest solution. Put your phone in airplane mode, hit the start button, and go.

Tracking

If you have limited downtime to devote to your goals or if your schedule is constantly changing, make vague appointments to work on your goals and track the time after the fact.

Limited Time. Set a few fifteen-minute appointments that repeat each week. Then, for instance, when you are waiting to pick your kids up from school, instead of checking social media, spend that time working on your alpha or beta project. Before you wrap up, go to the nearest calendar appointment, click into that time, and put in a few words about what you accomplished.

Changing Schedule. You can also set repeating appointments and track your time after the fact. I have a one-hour appointment in my calendar for every day at four in the afternoon. If I've spent the whole day working on clients and deadlines, it's time to work on my personal projects. Adhering to the 5 of 7 Rule, I keep the appointment at least five times a week. Then, I note in the description what I worked on that day.

This is why I like electronic calendars so much. If I already worked on my projects, I can just click and drag the appointment to the appropriate time from earlier in the day.

Journaling. There's that J word again. A journal really is the best way to compile your thoughts, note new ideas, and track your progress. Even a little time devoted to this each day is helpful.

In 2019, I made a commitment to start journaling every day. Granted, some days all I had time to write was lists of the things I did. On others, I went full-on anecdotal, detailing random conversations, ideas for articles, and people I met at events.

While you can and should schedule and track all of your commitments in a print and/or electronic calendar, a journal of everything you are doing adds value to this process. I keep my journal on Google Docs. Then, every three months, I save it on my computer and keep all the content together.

Even in the early stages of your goal projects, it's important to keep a log of what you have done, what you're doing, and how long each step takes. This allows you to review and reassess your progress at any time.

When you feel like you have *not* had a productive month, or even when you have, look at the appointments for a quick overview of what you accomplished. It'll remind you of how far you've come and will motivate you to keep going.

Chapter 20
Plan Rest Stops

Begin with the end in mind and where you want to stop along the way.

In the same way you would plan rest stops during a trip, you need to set deadlines for your goals. Rest stops might include lookout points, theme restaurants, and full-on tourist excursions. You should set deadlines for all tasks, benchmarks, and short-term goals. You can have an idea of your day of arrival to GoalTopia, but keep in mind that things don't always go as planned.

Put deadlines in your electronic calendar. Then set reminders to alert you when it's a week, two days, and the day before the deadline. You want to be able to meet your deadlines, so be realistic with your timing. If you think a short-term goal will take three months, give yourself four months to do it.

When I drove cross-country to Los Angeles, I started with the end in mind. I calculated how many hours of driving I'd do each day, where and when to stop, and I reserved hotel rooms accordingly. A thunderstorm in the first city threw my timing for a loop, I had plenty of planned and unplanned stops, and I got rerouted through Texas. But the map—and the integrity of the plan—remained.

You've done all the legwork. Now comes the fun part. It's time to take your goals, benchmarks, and tasks, and plan out your trip to GoalTopia.

Road Trip Exercise 20: Map Your Trip

Look at the big picture. Start with your long-term goals and work backward.

Be realistic about timing. You need to figure out your own time frame. Long-term goals can take one to five years or even a lifetime. Short-term goals can be accomplished in as little as one to six months.

Review your schedule. Before planning anything, look to see what is feasible. Arm yourself with mini-successes that will grow into major ones.

Set deadlines. You wouldn't be late on a project you are doing for someone else, would you? Set realistic deadlines. And keep them.

Batch tasks. Schedule time—and the steps—needed to accomplish your short-term goals. Also, look for commonalities, so your action items work together and you save time and energy.

Also, remember:

- Your trip will always take longer than anticipated.

- While day trips are part of the journey, beware of falling down rabbit holes.

- You will get there!

SECTION 5

Car Maintenance and Troubleshooting

There are potholes and detours on any road trip...or goal trip. Of course, some detours are good. Anyone interested in seeing the St. Louis Arch, enjoying a surprise celebrity concert at a county fair, or eating the largest commercially available pizza? (The pizza is in Texas, by the way, and bring friends.) Others are not so enjoyable. If you've ever gotten a flat tire, run out of gas, or been stuck visiting unfriendly relatives overnight, you know what I'm talking about.

Chapters 21 to 25 are all about strategies for navigating those bumps in the road and finding ways to enjoy the journey.

Be Prepared

Before you leave town, there are a few must-do items:

- Have the service station check your car. You want to be in tip top shape

- Fill your suitcases with the items you need, but leave space for the things you might pick up along the way

- Pack up your trunk, and don't forget your roadside assistance kit, spare tire, and gas can...just in case

- Bring snacks

- Wash your car. This is the automotive version of dress for success

Things Happen

During the course of your trip, anything could transpire.
You could:

- Get lost. Even with a complete map and plan, you may take a wrong turn somewhere

- Run out of gas. Sometimes you hit a long stretch with no service station in sight

- Have car trouble (because things happen)

- Get stuck (see above)

Good Distractions

- Not everything that happens on the road is bad. You could also:

- Make new friends, because you never know who you will meet during your journey

- Find great new resources, since not every place is on the map

- Discover a new town with lots to offer, so you want to stay an extra day or two

The Best Solution

Good or bad, whatever comes your way, embrace it, deal with it, and keep going.

Chapter 21
Create Rules and Rewards

Guidelines will keep you focused and on target.

One more thing to do before you turn on the ignition. Create rules and rewards for your journey.

Successful projects use some type of style sheet to keep all of the elements consistent and the process on track. You see these with books, podcasts, business proposals, employee manuals, and so on. So, we're going to set up rules for your journey, and talk about rewards you can receive when you accomplish certain goals.

Business Rules

Depending on your destination—whether it's happy employment, big business, or known expertise—you want to set rules for potential employers, clients, or your audience. You also want rules for your projects, as well as for yourself. That is where the rewards come into play.

When you know what attributes you want and need in your ideal situation, it's much easier to target, approach, and then make decisions.

Knowing what you are targeting also improves your networking. You are able to tell others exactly what you are looking for. And as you meet people with requirements different from yours, you can share resources. Make friends, form alliances, and refer them to others, since you are not in competition.

Employer Rules

Especially when leaving a bad work situation, you want to be hyper-aware of what will and will not work out. You do not want a repeat of what you are leaving.

Sara is looking for a new job. She wants to leave the large company she has been working at for the last four years. She has been passed up for promotions twice; she feels lost and unappreciated, and there is no room for growth.

Her previous company was a startup that went under. She was unemployed for six months, so she needs to find a job before she leaves this one. By exploring her options, she narrowed down the type of position and industry she is seeking. Further brainstorming will lead her to put together her preferred work environment.

Ideal company:

- Small to medium size business—private or public company

- No startups—at least five years old

- Tech, financial, or insurance industry

- Room for growth

- Ideal starting salary: $X

- Minimum starting salary: $X

- Full benefits

- Socially conscious

- Non-hostile work environment

- Less than 25 percent travel

Through research, she can identify some of the above: company size, salary range, benefits. This can aid her in knowing where to apply. Once she gets to the interview stage, she can learn more about the company and see how many of these boxes she can check.

She creates the following rules:

- Of the ten items on her list, four things are non-negotiable: No startups, room for growth, minimum salary, 25 percent travel

- The company needs to have at least six of her ideal characteristics

- And one benefit previously unknown

By creating rules, she can weed out what she does not want in a company so she does not end up in another unhappy situation.

Consultant Rules

To grow any business, you need a strong flow of new clients. Define your ideal client—make a list of ten attributes—so you know who to target. Determine size, budget, company culture, mission, philanthropies, and anything else you think might be relevant. As a result, it will be easier to hone your pitch, target your queries, ask for referrals, and, above all, develop your business.

Sam is a social media marketer who needs to grow his business or find a job working for someone else. Given his five years of experience, he knows exactly what type of person and company he prefers.

Ideal client:

- A medium-sized company
- Remote only
- Health and fitness industry
- One point of contact
- Is already tech savvy, so he doesn't have to educate them
- Community-minded
- Progressive
- Pays half the fee up front
- Has a budget of at least $10,000 per quarter
- Is willing to sign a three-month contract to start

This should give Sam a good starting point as he researches potential clients. Then, when he gets further along in the process, he can match his prospects' attributes to his list.

His rule is that any potential client must meet at least six of those requirements. However, what happens when a prospect meets six requirements and then has the following requests?

The client:

- Wants him on-site one day each week
- Has a slight learning curve when it comes to tech
- Wants to reduce his budget to $5,000
- He has to report to three different people

Those are big changes. Now, he has to rethink getting into business with this person.

Having rules about potential clients is a great barometer. If you find yourself compromising too much off the bat, it may signal a bunch of red flags. Be aware of them. When you and your client start mostly on the same page, it's more likely to lead to a mutually beneficial, long-term working relationship.

Audience and Buyer Rules

Targeting a person or a group of people is a little different than zeroing in on a business. In this case, you are looking for the attributes/characteristics/rules for your ideal buyer or audience member.

You may have already done some of this research in the journaling chapter, so you can refer to your notes. However, a fresh brainstorm can only serve to add details to the picture you are creating.

Ask yourself questions like:

- Who needs my product or service?

- Where do they live?

- What is my niche?

Then, write up a sketch—an avatar—that goes beyond demographics and specialty. Describe in as much detail as possible the type of person who wants to buy your product or service or hear you speak. This includes personality, values, and work ethic.

When doing your marketing, planning, or outreach, you will know who you are talking to.

Road Trip Exercise 21A: Business Rules

Make a list of attributes for your ideal business or client.

Or

Create an avatar for your ideal buyer or audience member.

Or

Both.

Refer to your notes and do additional brainstorming to create as complete a picture as possible.

Keep this list handy. And add a copy to your Trip Map.

Personal Rules

In addition to business specifics, you also want to have a list of rules or action items to refer to as you move forward on your road to GoalTopia. These are things you will do on a regular basis that will bring you closer to reaching your goals. They can relate to you, your projects, or your lifestyle changes.

For instance, you could write out how many days each week—and how much time per day—you will travel on your goal trip. Decide how many meetings you will take per week or month, as well as how much networking on behalf of the project you will do and how often.

Remember to include actions you will take to increase your personal well-being, which will help you with your professional aspirations. This can include working out, meditation, yoga, etc.

These are some of my favorite rules:

- **Become Your Biggest Fan.** Learn how to toot your own horn. Good promo starts with you.

- **Thinking Counts.** If you don't have time to work on it, make sure you spend time thinking about your project every day. However, thinking alone will not get your project done.

- **Take Breaks.** You know what they say about all work and no play... Schedule time to be social, work out, or meditate. It will help you stay refreshed and bring your A game.

- **Skills Improve with Practice.** If you are undertaking something new, don't be hard on yourself. The more you do it, the better you become.

- **Your Road Trip Should Be Fun.** If you are not enjoying what you are working on, it's likely no one else will, either. Bring your passion and enthusiasm to your work, so others can get excited too. *More on this in Chapter 25.*

Are you planning to write a book? Start a blog? Complete a home-improvement project? Or are you looking to find a hobby, take up a physical activity, or date more? You already have your itineraries. So assign rules to keep these projects in forward motion.

For instance:

- **For a book:** Outline during week one, write one chapter a week, then, after you have a complete draft, edit one chapter a week

- **For a blog:** Write X blog posts a month, post on social media X times a week

- **For home improvement:** Spend X hours on a project each Saturday; once completed, celebrate, take a week off, then repeat with the next project

- **For a hobby:** Try a different hobby each month until you find one you like

- **For physical activity:** Try a different form of exercise each month until you find one you like

- **For dating:** Spend X hours a week on a dating site or app. Schedule X new dates a month

Rules are personal, so you have to adapt them to your capabilities. For example, Travis is writing a book, but his health issues are making it a challenge since he cannot type that fast or that long. He has tried voice-to-text, but there are still things he needs to write out. His rule is five hundred words a week. Sometimes he can get it done by Tuesday, other times, not until the end of the week. It may not seem like a lot, but it's a goal he can hit. And he is making progress.

Road Trip Exercise 21B: Personal Rules

Make a list of personal rules.

Or

Make a list of project rules.

Or

Both.

Note your rules in your calendar and add a copy to your Trip Map. Keep the rules you set.

Solopreneur Work-From-Home Rules

Cassie is an accountant who works from home. Since she needs to make marketing a priority, she balances it with her client responsibilities. To stay productive and make sure nothing falls through the cracks, Cassie created daily, weekly, monthly, and quarterly rules for herself.

Daily

- Networking: Follow up with at least one client (five per week)

- Exercise: fifteen minutes

- Get dressed & ready for the day (no working in PJs)

Weekly

- Networking: one event/coffee/lunch

- Exercise: one or two outings: tennis, golf, walk on the beach

Quarterly (one of each)

- Newsletter

- Freelance article

- Speaking engagement

The Rewards

Sure, reaching GoalTopia will be a reward in and of itself, but there's nothing wrong with scheduling incentives along the way. Decide what types of rewards you will receive for reaching benchmarks, short-term, and long-term goals.

For example:

- **Rule:** Go to four networking events each month
- **Reward:** Every two months, take a week off

- **Rule:** Publish a new podcast each week
- **Reward:** After each twelve-week season, celebrate with a special dinner out

- **Rule:** Spend X hours a week on goal trip
- **Reward:** After every milestone, a treat; after every short-term goal achieved, staycation weekend; after every long-term goal achieved, vacation

Road Trip Exercise 21C: Rewards

Assign rewards for following each rule.

Add them to your Trip Map.

Enjoy them.

Rewards

Here some of the most popular—and in some cases very specific—rewards, which are combined from my clients, my community, and the Goal Survey.

- Food and Drink: Fancy coffee, special food, dark chocolate, martinis

- Pampering: Bubble bath, lavender oil, sleeping in

- Family: Celebration with spouse or partner, enjoying a fun family activity

- Treats: New books, stationary, shoes, clothes, a shopping spree

- Time off: Vacation, staycation, a weekend break

Note: Some people prefer to assign penalties for not reaching their weekly goals, and that is definitely an option. For instance, you can put money in a jar when you miss the deadlines for your goals and then donate it.

However, I think celebrating successes is much more motivating. It keeps you excited about your goal trip at every stop.

I am definitely more of the gold star, give everyone a trophy, celebrate all wins—even-the-small-ones—type.

Chapter 22

Deal with Detours, Roadblocks, and Car Trouble

The best way to deal with the unexpected is to roll with it.

Crashing through roadblocks only makes sense in the movies or on TV. In real life, you have to actually deal with the things that throw you for a loop. In fact, *life* is probably the biggest disruption to pursuing goals.

You can plan your trip down to the last detail, and, still, things may—will—go wrong. This chapter shows you how to deal with them.

Detours

When I was growing up, my mom loved taking shortcuts. If there was a way to avoid excess traffic, she would take it. The thing about shortcuts—or detours—is that sometimes they work out to your benefit. You find a local hidden treasure, make a new friend, or see a beautiful landscape you would never have discovered otherwise. However, other times, all that detour does is take you off course.

Shiny Object Syndrome

The main reason for setting up a personal or professional motto is to help you determine which backroads serve your goals and which ones to avoid. When unexpected opportunities present themselves, don't take that highway exit immediately. Pull over to a rest stop, check your compass, and see if it will keep you going in the right direction.

Ask yourself:

- Will doing this help me get to GoalTopia?

- Is there something that I can reprioritize to make room to do this?

- Will this opportunity present itself again? Or must I act now?

- Does this count as a reward or a fun break?

- Will doing this make me happy? Or am I doing it for someone else? (It is fine if it's for someone else's benefit, it just has to be for yours, too.)

Opinions of Others

This is your journey. Don't let anyone else navigate for you.

Everyone is going to have an opinion on how you live your life—it's human nature—but it doesn't mean they get a say. Some people may be your champions and may offer you good advice. Even when that's the case, you don't want to consult too many people. Differing opinions may mean getting torn into too many directions.

Most people, however, are not objective. They may mean well, but they could be jealous, having a bad day, or just frustrated with their own life. In any case, they are acting from their own experience and point of view, not yours.

Cynthia, who is at an employment crossroads, is having a hard time deciding her next step. This is primarily because everyone in her life has given her different advice about what she should do.

Her cousin said, "Start a business. Find something you can easily market and sell that."

Her sister said, "Do consulting. You love consulting."

And her brother said, "Get a job. Consultants don't make any money." Cynthia feels torn in each possible direction, and for good reason.

My response, "Take the time to figure out what it is you really want. And then talk only to people who support you. To everyone else, say, 'Thank you. I appreciate your opinion.' Then change the subject as quickly as possible."

Here's the thing. Only you know your personal, employment, and financial situation. There may be someone else who is a fundamental part of your life—a partner or a spouse, kids—and they may deserve to share their opinion. But you get to make the final decision.

Self-Doubt

You've made a choice to change your life, you've done the leg work to figure out what you want, so trust yourself. I believe in you!

Is something stopping you from achieving your goals? Or are you choosing detours that take you off the right path?

When the block is yourself and the detour is you going in circles, the best thing you can do is re-center yourself. Go back to your Trip Map, review your visualization, your mission, and motto, and see if they still ring true and if your roadmap supports it. If so, keep going.

Still confused? Go back to Directed Journaling. Over the next few days, write out why you are experiencing these feelings of self-doubt, and then look at them objectively. In the best-case scenario, you will get the feelings out of your head and your heart and will feel clear enough to continue on your path.

Alternatively, you may pinpoint where your challenges are— perhaps you need different resources, more education, or additional support. Maybe you are overwhelmed and exhausted from something going on in your personal life, and you need some rest or some fun to replenish your soul. In those cases, plan a detour that fills those holes, after which you can get back on track.

Roadblocks

Wouldn't it be nice to have endless time, boundless energy, and abundant money to support your road trip? You could drive straight through from your current location to your destination and get there so much faster. But as you know, that's not how life works. Even if all of the above were true, there are still things beyond your power that may get in your way.

Work

Whether or not your primary source of income is related to your goal trip, there are times when work will be a priority. Urgent things come up, deadlines get moved, your workload increases. However, there may come a point—whether you work for yourself or others—when you need to set boundaries.

For example:

- Don't check work email or answer calls after seven in the evening during the week

- Only check work email twice on the weekends, and no phone calls unless it's an emergency

- When you take days off, set an out-of-office message on your email

In order to make progress on your goals, you need to make—and take—the time.

Family

Ah, family. Depending on your home situation, you probably spend a decent amount of time with your immediate family: dinners, weekends, and the occasional outing. You also probably see extended family regularly for holidays, visits, and whatnot.

The most common problem I see with my clients and community, especially freelancers, is they have family members who don't understand what they are doing and why. They either try to take advantage of a freelancer's flexible schedule, or they mistake a side hustle for a hobby. If it's not bringing you a lot of immediate income, it doesn't count, right? Wrong.

Does this sound familiar?

- "You can pick up the kids from school, right? You don't have a meeting like I do."

- "Can you go to the store, buy these things for Grandma, and then make the hour drive to bring them to her?"

- "Why can't you come with me to my kid's school play? You're not actually working."

Kind of like with work, you need to set boundaries with family. Except these boundaries are for them, not you. So that they are less likely to take advantage of your good nature, give your extended family limited windows of time when you can offer additional support or join them for activities. Be firm, but friendly, when you tell them, "No." More on that in Chapter 24. Every now and then, you may want to make an exception. That's fine, as long as it's your choice...and it's not the rule.

Things You Can't Control

And then there are things you can do little about such as illness, family emergencies, and other personal issues. Even natural disasters and long-term power outages can have an impact on your goals. When that happens, all bets are off. You go into survival mode.

The distraction doesn't even have to be something devastating. Sometimes life gets in the way. This happened quite literally to my client S. Latria. We started working together on her book edits a few months after her youngest was born. We had a few sessions where I gave her recommendations for her writing process—balancing—and some developmental suggestions. Then, she hit the pause button.

About a year later, I got an email from her. S. Latria wrote that she had taken on too much at once, struggling to become a writer while adjusting to being a stay-at-home mom of two. Instead of dialing it back, she convinced herself she wasn't a writer at all. It took her a while, but she was able to reroute and believe in herself again.

S. Latria told me she continued to edit her book, but at a much slower pace. And, when she hit a roadblock (her words), she worked on other creative projects. That combination helped her focus on improving her work as well. I'm thrilled to say she is back on track to self-publish this fall. Every time I see her posting about her upcoming release, it makes me smile.

It just goes to show that when life throws you into a tailspin, all you can do is get through it. When things settle out, take a breath and forgive yourself for being stalled. Then, regroup, reset your deadlines, and move forward. Your goal trip may take a little longer, but you'll get there.

Car Trouble

Car won't start? Got a flat tire? Overheated engine? Any way you look at it, you are stuck. Sometimes, you are waiting for someone to do their part so you can move forward. Other times, you are just plain stalled. That's why it's important to have alpha and beta projects so something is always in motion.

When you find yourself standing still, it's likely because you have a creative or productivity block, you don't know what to do next, or you just need to get out of your head. There's still plenty you can do to make use of your free moments and get unstuck while you are waiting for the tow truck to arrive.

Wait in the Car

These first five you can do in long or short periods of time. If you are early to an appointment, waiting for a late lunch companion, or stuck in a long line, try one of these.

Choose Something Random. Jot a list of all the low-maintenance, minimal time-commitment things that need to be done on your goal trip. Then pick one at random to do on the spot. Can't decide? Go with the close your eyes and point method. Bonus: You can also do this for outreach and networking. Make a list of people you have been meaning to contact, pick one at random, and reach out.

Low-Commitment Tasks. Go through your to-do list and select an action item you can start and finish in one sitting. For example, write a marketing letter, rewrite your bio, or sketch up a new or revised product design. If your long-term project is going to take a while, it's nice to have a feeling of accomplishment. Every small victory adds up. That sense of completion will keep you motivated and keep your mind active and focused as take on your more challenging—and more time-consuming—goals!

Journaling. When was the last time you updated your tracking document with progress on your trip? Take a few minutes to scribble some notes. You can also do some free-form brain dumping. Write what's on your mind, what needs to be done, what challenges you're facing. Often, the writing process will produce solutions. And, remember, doodling also counts.

Educate Yourself. Whatever your goal trip, there's always plenty to learn. Find or take a class, check out an industry website, listen to podcasts or audiobooks, or read a book about your niche or industry. It's essential to keep up on trends in your area of interest. Find experts and see what they have to say.

Disconnect. Put your smartphone away and take a few minutes to breathe and refocus. Especially when you're on the verge of feeling overwhelmed, it's important to step back and maybe even meditate before you spiral. Sit quietly, listen to music, or do some people-watching; that always makes for a fun game.

Park the Car

When you are feeling really stifled, it could mean that you need to take an actual break. Here are five things you can do to get out of your head when you have a bit more time on your hands. Trust me, you will be more productive later.

Exercise. While taking a walk every now and then is just good sense, a regular exercise regimen will help you improve your mental and physical health; you will feel better about yourself and things in general. And it may be even be a beta goal. Most gyms—including your local YMCA—offer free trials. Some fitness studios allow you to pay for one class at a time at intro prices before committing to a series. You can also go for a run, a bike ride, a swim, or change up your exercise regimen each month: kickboxing one month, aerobics the next, and so on. Once you decide what sort of exercise to explore, commit to doing it once or twice a week. Note: You do not need to get *stuck* to start exercising.

Do Something Creative. When working on any sort of project, it's helpful to view things from a different perspective. One of the best ways to accomplish that is to do something creative. Even better, come up with a project that's the opposite of your natural tendencies. If you like things tidy, paint something free-form. If you think you can't draw, draw a picture anyway. Take photos, write a poem, or make something. The finished product doesn't have to be good; just have fun! Whatever the medium, it will stir up those creative juices and send you back to pursuing your goals with a fresh perspective.

Take a Dance Break. Those of you who work in a traditional office (especially a trendy, communal workspace) may have a little trouble doing this, but see what you can do. For those who work at home, there are no excuses. When you're stuck, instead of having a shot of caffeine, give dancing a shot. Turn on some music, crank up the volume, and let loose. (Yes, I do this regularly.) Not comfortable dancing? Fine. Just turn up the tunes and sing along or zone out for a few. It's amazing how refreshed you will feel before getting back to the task at hand.

Cook Dinner. Are you one of those healthy eaters? A professional snacker? Maybe you're someone who only eats on the go? Mix things up and prepare a meal that's different from your norm. You don't need to be a gourmet cook, and comfort food totally counts. If you don't already have a favorite recipe, search for one on the internet, make a list of ingredients, go shopping, and cook. Many people find cooking relaxing. You could be one of them. Secret tip: I was never much of a cook until I got an Instant Pot (pressure cooker) a couple of years ago. I love it because you prepare and add ingredients, set it to go, and then accomplish other things while it's cooking. In my experience, the results have been delicious.

Take Time Off. During your travel on your goal trip, you will work too hard. Take the next exit and enjoy a complete break. See a movie. Have lunch or dinner out...or in. Go to karaoke night. It's just as important to schedule downtime as it is to get things accomplished. If downtime is not a personal goal, maybe it should be. Remember, everything will get done. Remain mindful of your route, keep moving forward, and take care of yourself.

If you are truly stuck and can't seem to move forward on one or any of your projects, you have three options:

- **Park.** Put a pin in what's been challenging you and come back to it in a month or two. The timing may not be right.

- **Neutral.** Every day, 5 of 7, spend a few minutes focused on what is stumping you. If you are a musician, play the scales. If you are an artist, doodle. If you are developing a product or business, brainstorm. Get it the habit of thinking about it; solutions and progress will eventually present themselves.

- **Reverse.** Go back to Chapter 1 and start again. You may be on the wrong road.

You know how sometimes when you leave the house a little late because you got sidetracked, and then pass a car accident, you wonder if you missed it because you ran late? In my family, we call situations like that "Tuesday." It's our reminder that when plans change, there's a reason.

On a Tuesday, last winter, I was bound and determined to go to my morning dance class even though thing after thing went wrong.

"I didn't sleep well. That's okay, I'll go anyway," I said. "I have that deadline. That's okay, I'll have so much energy from dancing, I will write it in no time," I said. And then...

"The heater went out. I have to call the landlord. Okay, I get it. No dance class for me today," I acquiesced. At the time of my dance class, I received a call asking me to come in earlier for an important meeting. Had I been at class, I would have missed the call and had to reschedule my meeting for another month.

The thing to remember with any of these blockages is that everything will work out the way it's supposed to, whether you like it or not.

Chapter 23
Find a Support System

Building a strong foundation includes aligning
yourself with the right people.

An important step in achieving goals is discovering your tribe:
those who understand you, support you, and help propel you.
You can't achieve your goals on your own. You need clients
and prospects to buy from you, mentors and experts to educate
you, students and peers to learn from you, and so on. You also
need trusted advisors and a friendly community to lead you and
cheer you on.

The people you meet, both on and off the road—and on- and
offline—may not even be your strongest connections. But they
could know people who fall into one of the aforementioned
categories. The more you prioritize growing your network, the
quicker you will develop relationships with those excited to
help you succeed.

Speaking of people who want you to succeed...put me at the top
of that list.

Live Networking

No matter your destination, networking goals should be an
integral part of your route. My general rule of thumb is to
participate in one live networking experience every week,
whether it's a group mixer, meeting, continuing education

event, or a one-on-one breakfast, lunch, or coffee. Based on what you do, where you live, and what you want, you will find a variety of possibilities.

Discover and Attend Events

While the majority of events are after work, some organizations do breakfast and lunch meetups. Events include speed networking and mixers, book signings and seminars, special interest and hobby excursions, workshops and conferences, and more.

In larger cities, opportunities are everywhere. On most nights, there are at least two or three competing events. If you live in a smaller town, you may have to look a little harder to find something worthwhile to attend, but there will be options. Go to MeetUp or Eventbrite. Check your local library, bookstore, or coworking space, if you have one. Or do a good old-fashioned local internet search.

An even better way to discover events is to ask your friends and associates for recommendations. Message your contacts directly or pose the question to your LinkedIn network. You want to find meetings related to your specialty, of course, for comradery and education. However, it's also important to find more general groups or events slightly out of your niche, since they're better for prospecting. Being a website designer in a group of other techies may not net you clients unless a peer has overflow work to share. Being a designer at a Chamber of Commerce mixer might be more useful for client development.

Also consider attending business-related educational events—marketing, social media, accounting, app development—to help you up-level your knowledge base and pique your curiosity.

Starting a new project, career, or venture is all about taking risks. Dip your toes in the water and try something a little different from your norm. Plus, when you break out of your regular box, the people you meet can introduce you to entirely new communities.

Note: If the cost of an event is prohibitive, offer your services as a volunteer. You will get to meet a lot more people, have better access to speakers, and have an easy conversation-starter.

Another way to meet new people and grow your community through events is to become a speaker, either by yourself or as part of a panel. Even if the Big City is not your destination, there's no reason you can't share your expertise locally. Come up with a list of subjects you can speak on as well as some panel ideas (topics and fellow speakers). Then, make a list of conferences or local groups where you'd want to speak. Search the websites or email for submission guidelines. Craft your pitch, send it, and follow through.

Connect

Don't let those new business contacts fall through the cracks. Exchange business cards or contact information with all of your new peeps.

Whether you're a speaker, attendee, or volunteer, follow up with everyone you meet at an event. Ideally, write a simple, personalized note and send a LinkedIn connection request within forty-eight hours. Since it is business-centric, many people will connect on LinkedIn instead of other social networks.

And if you want to connect with me on LinkedIn, feel free: LinkedIn.com/in/Coastbunny. Just remember to include a note.

Developing Relationships on LinkedIn

Whenever I meet someone at a business-centric event, LinkedIn is my first stop. It's fun to see if we have any mutual connections. And outside of real life, LinkedIn really is the best way to get to know someone new. It's designed that way.

Your LinkedIn profile enables you to compose an intro—what you do and how you help others—along with education, experiences, skills, etc. There are also places for people to endorse and recommend you, as well as ample opportunities to post content—including live and pre-recorded video—interact, and expand your network. And that's just skimming the surface.

One of the best ways to get noticed on LinkedIn, and remind connections of who you are, is to post regular updates. This includes live and pre-recorded video. If you are comfortable in front of the camera, nothing beats video for showcasing who you are and what you know along with your personality.

Here are five more things you can post as updates on LinkedIn.

1. An Article or Blog Post. Whenever you have a new article, whether it's on your blog or another website, share the link with your connections. Be sure to add an image so it stands out. If the piece is for another site, an interview or a round-up post, be sure to use the @ to tag anyone mentioned, so they are notified and can share your post.

2. News. One of the most important things about being an expert in your industry is staying on top of the latest developments, trends, and news. If there is anything going on related to your field (a new product launch or update, a scientific advancement, etc.), find a relevant article and share it with your people.

3. Expert Advice. Don't just share your own articles. Find posts from others in your industry that will be helpful for your connections. Remember, you don't need to know everything. You just need to find reliable sources to share information regularly. Again, @ tag anyone whose post you share. And always reply to comments on your updates.

4. Events. Attending or speaking at a local event? Let your connections know. As I've already mentioned, nothing beats a real-live meet. Be sure to take some photos that you can post after the fact on LinkedIn and your other social networks.

5. Questions. Whether you need a good place to have a meeting, resources for your goal trip, or quotes for a blog post, just ask your people. Questions serve as great conversation starters. And, as a bonus, the more engagement you get (responses, likes, and shares), the more active your post will be in the feed.

For everything you need to know on LinkedIn, search for articles by Viveka Von Rosen of Vengreso. She is my favorite resource on the subject.

You can also follow people on Twitter and Instagram and support their business pages on Facebook. If they have YouTube channels, subscribe. Your show of support will be appreciated and may even be reciprocated.

Social Media

One of the best things about social media is that it can help you solidify relationships with people you just met in real life and vice versa. When you go to an event, you will meet a lot of people in a short period of time. Use social as an opportunity to get to know your connections better and see which contacts develop into business relationships and which of them become actual friends. Whenever you make a solid business or social connection, make plans to meet in-person to continue the conversation.

Online Groups and Chats

Event networking works the other way around as well. Many events, especially the larger ones, will have a hashtag or group you can connect with prior to the event. Participate ahead of time. Make friends in the group and then make a point to meet in real life. And if you can't go to a live event (due to financial or geographic circumstances), find an event to attend online. They are typically less expensive and still offer networking opportunities—Facebook groups, message boards, webinars— between virtual attendees.

Note: If you ever find yourself questioning an online-only connection—you feel something is off—go with your gut. See if there's anyone you know in common, and then drop a note to a mutual friend, asking how they know this person. Most people are genuine, but it doesn't hurt to verify that people are who they say they are.

Also use social media to discover new communities that may or may not be associated with IRL events. Find where your people hang out and join the conversation. Check out LinkedIn and

Facebook groups relevant to your industry as well as Twitter chats. You can also join alumni groups and groups related to a hobby. Much like when you search for events, ask peers for group recommendations. You can also do an internet search—or search through the platform—with your topic and the social network to see what comes up.

Twitter Chats

Want to step up your game on Twitter and find new communities? Explore Twitter chats. They are a great way to meet new people, learn new things, and expand your network.

What Is a Twitter Chat? A Twitter chat is a conversation on Twitter designated by a particular hashtag. It usually revolves around a certain topic and is hosted by the same person or group of people at the same time every week. While some are run by big brands, many are organized by individuals (experts, consultants, bloggers) who share a passion for a particular topic.

Many Twitter chats have special guests who answer questions from the hosts. The format is simple. Q1 with a question is tweeted and people reply with A1 and then the response. Attendees are welcome to add their two cents—280 characters—as well.

To see all the tweets from a chat, do a Twitter search for the hashtag and select, "Latest Tweets," or use a website such as Hootsuite or TweetDeck. For the latter, simply add a column with the hashtag you want to follow to see all the tweets.

How to Find Twitter Chats. There are some Twitter chat directories, like TweetReports. Search the page for one of your keywords or read through the lists to see what appeals to you. Another way to find a specific type of Twitter chat is to simply search your topic of interest and then "Twitter Chat." For instance, search for "Twitter Chats Writing" or

"Marketing Twitter Chats," and you will find lists of top chats on the topic. If you search "Twitter Chats Goals," my "#GoalChat" will come up. Madalyn Sklar, who hosts the #TwitterSmarter Twitter chat on Thursdays at 10:00 a.m. PST, has a curated list of Twitter chats for marketers, content, and business professionals on MadalynSklar.com.

Once you find a few chats that interest you, test them out. Make appointments with yourself to try one or two chats a week until you land on a few good ones to join regularly, so you develop relationships similar to how you would in an in-person group.

Chat Etiquette. Before you get started, here are a few things to keep in mind.

- Follow the hosts. This is something you can do before you even get to a chat. Find the hosts, follow them, and tweet that you are looking forward to their chat. You may want to retweet some of their tweets prior to the chat.

- Follow the guests. And if they give you other ways to connect like on LinkedIn, you might as well do that, too. Just add a note that you met them on this chat.

- Introduce yourself. Usually at the beginning of the chat, the host allows time for you to introduce yourself with some sort of ice breaker. Jump on in.

- Observe. You may just want to read the tweets your first chat or two. As I previously mentioned, attendees are typically welcome to reply. However, depending on how fast the chat is, you may find it easier to watch the chat and retweet the responses that mirror your beliefs.

- Engage. Once you are comfortable, answer questions and reply to others in the chat. You will likely want to follow the other attendees and continue your Twitter conversations outside of the chat.

Once you find the online groups that suit you, be active without being self-promotional. This means adding value: share information (showcasing your expertise), answer questions, and reply to comment threads. You never know when you will strike up a conversation with someone who could be a potential client down the line.

Social Networking

The same way you put yourself on an IRL (in real life) networking schedule, create one for keeping in touch online. Schedule a fifteen-minute appointment with yourself at least once a week to jot notes to people with whom you have lost touch. You can even spend your first fifteen-minute session making a list of such people.

Here's what you can do:

Say Hi. You can reply to or comment on a milestone, new job, or promotion as listed on Facebook or LinkedIn. Or simply send a short IM or email: "Hi *Person*. Been ages. How's everything going? How's your *significant other/family/business*? Fill me in on what you've been up to when you have a chance."

Remember, this isn't about what you need. It's about putting yourself back in the minds of others. Opportunities may arise from conversations to work together or help each other out. But you're more likely to think of someone (and vice versa), if you have recently been in touch.

Bonus: Jump on the phone or do a video chat. Nothing beats a verbal or face-to-face catch-up to remind people of who you are and what you do.

Make a Request. There's value in asking for what you need. Ask a friend, colleague, or business contact for a referral, testimonial, or introduction. Then, offer to do the same for this person and/or someone else.

Sometimes it's intimidating or uncomfortable to ask for help. Don't worry so much! Reasonable requests should never be a problem. People love to help. Besides, when you don't ask, the answer is always, "No."

Connect Your Contacts. Business is all about referrals. Your friends and peers can benefit from the skills, experience, and advice of others. Make some connections. Look through your Facebook or LinkedIn feeds and see if one of your friends posted that they need something. See if you can help. Or, if you know someone who can fulfill that need, introduce them. *Just make sure you ask before sharing someone's email address.*

By the way, you don't always need to wait for someone to ask for something to make an intro. Go through your list of friends and connections, decide which of your trusted troupe would benefit from meeting another member, and make an intro.

Facebook Groups

While most of your professional contacts may be on LinkedIn, Facebook is also a viable place to develop and be part of a community.

There is a group for every specialty. You just have to look, search, and get recommendations.

Before joining a group, read the rules. Some are very specific about how and when they allow self-promotion.

Before friending or accepting a friend request from someone in a group, check out their profile. Look for images and see if you have any mutual connections. You want to connect with real people, not salesy ones.

Don't see a community that fits your niche? Or just want to start one? Go for it.

To create a group:

- Click, "Create" at the top and select, "Group"

- Name your group

- Assign privacy

- Add image and details

- Include guidelines in your description

- Select settings

- Invite friends

- Post regularly

- Add managing a Facebook group to your goals

If you can't find like minds nearby, create your own inviting environment.

Remember, the keyword in social networking is, "Social." If you are friendly, authentic, and professional on whatever platforms you use, you will develop genuine relationships with like minds.

Accountability

That takes care of resources to help propel your goals forward, but what about you? Accountability is a key motivational element in completing your goals. What will keep you on track with your goals? Other than my mantra of, "You can do it," on repeat in your head.

The Buddy System

Find a friend or group of friends, and make an appointment to check in at the same time every week. These can be five-minute appointments. Get in, check in, and go back to work. The biggest challenge, of course, is finding someone supportive, who knows what you are going through, and is out for your best interests. That's why it is optimal to choose a buddy who is also working toward their goals. You want to be tailgating cross-country. Backseat drivers only hamper the progress.

Family Goals

Do you have a supportive family? Are they enthusiastic about making changes and getting things done? Why not make goals a family project?

While you are working on your goal trip, encourage your partner, parents, kids, whomever to take on a project of their own. Or work on a project together. Then, every week, have a family meeting to review your progress.

To keep things positive and productive, set some ground rules:

- Everyone gets three to five minutes to report on their goals and set new ones

- Only supportive, positive comments are allowed

- No unsolicited directions unless someone requests feedback

- Save a few minutes at the end for general questions

Take your loved ones along for the ride. They will have a better understanding of what you are working toward and may offer tips for a smoother trip.

My Communities

Around 2008, shortly after I joined Facebook. I added an online community for my live writers' support group. The Write On Online Facebook page was based on the same principles as the live group: Tell people what you are going to do, and you are more likely to do it. So, at the beginning of every week, I ask people to share their goals and, at the end of the week, to report on how they did.

When I first started doing this, they weren't always the same people. Members would share what they are planning to do, but not report back. Or if someone had an outstanding week, they would share what they accomplished without initially sharing a goal. Both of these scenarios are fine, by the way. I want people to be thinking about and sharing goals at any stage. And if you are concerned about privacy, you don't need to share the details. A time, page, word, or general benchmark goal will do the trick.

A few years ago, I revitalized the Facebook group that is attached to the Write On page. Although everyone thinks it's still solely a writers' support group, it's more of a people's support group. It's aimed at writers, creatives, and entrepreneurs since, in this age where entrepreneurs must be writers and creatives, and writers and creatives must also be entrepreneurs—a.k.a. marketers—there is a lot of overlap.

This community gives members prompts to share and encourage almost every day. Mondays are networking goals, Tuesdays are weekly goals, and Wednesdays are blog share day. Then, there is Toot Your Horn Thursday and Foto Friday (both self-explanatory). Saturdays ask about weekend plans. There are monthly threads as well as other opportunities to share what you are working on and how you can help others in the group.

My favorite example of this was when one member asked if anybody knew any audiobook readers. I remembered someone mentioning on a previous Toot Your Horn Thursday that she just set up her home recording studio for her voice-over business. An introduction was made. When you put who you are and what you do out there, you never know what may come of it.

In January 2018, I decided to pull the trigger on launching my Twitter chat. #GoalChat is Sunday at 7:00 p.m. PST. You can see how long that goal was on my list because I got the GoalChat Twitter account in May 2013. I wanted to expand my social reach beyond my Facebook community since not everyone is active on the platform. What was originally just going to be a goal check-in turned into a full-blown Twitter chat after just two weeks.

That model, which I still use, is this:

- Introduce yourselves

- Q1. What was your biggest win last week?

- Q1b. How did you do on your health and fitness goals?

- Q2. What are your goals for the week?

And then we delve into a special topic, which usually has a business, social media, productivity, or work-life balance spin. Once a month, we do monthly goals. Annual goals are at the beginning of the year. And we have a virtual holiday party each December.

The community are the guests. They show up every week to encourage each other and offer their expertise on whatever we are talking about. And the best part is I have never met any of my regulars in real life, not yet, anyway.

If you are reading this book, it goes without saying, but I'll say it anyway: I would be delighted if you would join any or all of my communities.

Chapter 24
Maintain Balance

If you feel balanced more than half of the time, you are doing better than most.

When was the last time you aligned your tires? Or yourself?

Work-life balance—or is life-work balance?—is the ultimate challenge for busy professionals. You can't give 100 percent to everything all the time. There are only a certain number of hours in the day to divide between work, family, sleep, eating, errands, exercise, etc. When you add new goals to the mix, it may be challenging to rearrange and maintain that balance. But you can do it!

While you may never be in perfect harmony all the time, there are tactics you can employ to create a lifestyle that works for you.

Finding Balance

Work-life balance is having enough time to do the things you want to do and still accomplish everything you have to do.

Before you can have balance in your life, decide what that means for you.

Ask yourself:

- How many hours of sleep do you need a night to feel balanced?

- How much family time do you want/need in a day? In a week? In a month?

- How much downtime do you need each week? How much downtime do you actually get? What does downtime mean? Are you taking care of yourself? Or should that be a goal?

- Does work make you happy? Or are you going on this goal trip to find a better work situation?

- How much time do you put into work each week? Is there wiggle-room? Can you set better boundaries?

- Will the pockets of time for your goal trip take from work time, play time, or sleep? Is that a doable solution?

- Does your goal trip feel like play? Does it make you happy enough that it gives you hope for a better future?

Review your answers to see how you can best redistribute your time to make room for your goal trip.

Downtime

Whenever you are working toward your goals, no matter what they may be, you should schedule downtime to help you maintain a sense of self as well as personal balance. You can't be cruising down the highway, full speed ahead, all the time.

Take out your calendar and do the following:

- Make ongoing appointments with yourself in the morning, mid-day, or evening.

- Schedule these a few minutes every day or in larger chunks of time once a week.

- If you have to move an appointment for downtime around, that's fine. Just don't delete it.

For these self-care breaks, you can find inspiration for getting unstuck in the Car Trouble section of Chapter 22. Or come up with some ideas of your own.

Make a list of fifty things you can do that would make you happy.

- Ten things you can do in fifteen minutes or less

- Ten things you can do in an hour or less

- Ten things you can do in a free morning or afternoon

- Ten things you can do in a day

- Ten things you can do in two or more days; think staycation or vacation

Some of these can be considered rewards as discussed in Chapter 21, which is fine. But note which ones should be mandatory self-care. If you want to continue balancing everything, you need to stay healthy. When you are healthy, you have a clearer mind and are much more productive. You are also a better asset to your family and friends.

Saying "No"

I can't mention balance without addressing this subject. People constantly tell me that one of the reasons they do not have time for themselves or their goals is that they feel obligated to help others. While being altruistic is important—remember your mission?—at some point, you need to give yourself the same consideration you give others and put yourself first.

One way to find time for a more balanced life is to learn to say, "No."

Have any of these scenarios happened to you?

School Daze

PTA Mom: "Can you help with the school committee?"

You: "Well, I have a huge deadline at the end of the month, so I can't really devote the time."

PTA Mom: "But you are so good at promotion. It'll only be a few hours a week."

You: "A few hours?"

PTA Mom: "Well, less than twenty total, but you are speedy, so it will probably won't take you that long."

What you want to say: "No."

What you say: "Yes."

What happens: You dedicate more than forty hours because when she said "help," she meant "lead" the committee, and everyone else shirked their responsibilities. You are not happy with the work you have done for either project. Plus, you are frustrated, sleep-deprived, and mad at yourself for not sticking to your instincts.

What you should have said: "I understand that volunteering is part of my responsibilities as a parent at the school. However, the timing is not great. Let's take a look at the calendar and pick something I can contribute in the near future. I will be less stressed, won't have to split my focus, and will do a better job on both projects."

Or this?

Chauffeur Duty

Adult Son: "Mom, will you pick up your grandchild from school this afternoon and take him over to the dentist?"

You: "I'd love to help you out, but you know this is my designated writing day."

Adult Son: "I know it's short notice, but I have a meeting for work."

You: "You know your schedule. Why did you double-book?"

Adult Son: "The work thing was last minute. You'd really be helping me out. And I know how much you two enjoy spending time together."

Ahhh. Guilt.

What you want to say: "No."

What you say: "Yes."

What happens: You do it. It's fine. But you get the same request a week later. Then, when you try to say, "No," the response is, "But you did it last time, and didn't you two have the best time?"

What you should have said: "I understand it's last minute, and I will help you out this time. But in the future, I'd appreciate it if you would find an alternative. Even though it's freelance, it's still work; I cannot skip all the time." Optional: "I take Fridays off, so if you need me to pick him up on a Friday, that's much easier."

Or this?

Panel Predicament

Event Organizer: "Do you want to be on a panel for this cool—but not related at all to your business goals—event? We had a last-minute cancellation and we'd love to bring you on board."

What you want to say: "No."

What you say: "Yes."

What happens: This could go either way.

- You do the event; you don't really get work out of it, but you do make some nice connections.

- You do the event. It went okay, but it's definitely not a topic you would speak on in the future. It felt strained, but you pulled it off. To top it off, you discover the topic that is your forte is on the schedule for three months from now, and you are not eligible since they have a rule against repeating speakers within a year.

What you should have said: "I'd love to help out. But just so you know this is more on the cusp of my niche. My true expertise is X. Whether or not I am still a fit for this event, I'd appreciate it if you would think of me the next time my topic comes up, regardless of the timing."

To avoid—or at least lessen—regret, wasted time, and
frustration, before you commit to anything, ask yourself
three questions:

- What is the benefit? Will it help me professionally,
  personally, or both? Does it reflect my mission?

- What is the commitment? Do I have the time and
  bandwidth to take this on? Will it take away from my
  downtime? Is that okay with me?

- Do you want to do it? When it comes right down to it,
  this is really the only answer that matters.

When making a decision to do—or not do—something, consider
yourself and your other obligations first. Granted, emergencies
happen and sometimes the choice is a clear, "Yes." However,
if your answer is, "No," mean it, stick to it, and keep any
(necessary) explanation short and firm.

Think of saying, "No," as giving yourself the gift of time,
whether you use it for downtime, work time, or family time.

Chapter 25
Enjoy Your Adventure

Use your passion as fuel for your journey.

You plan and take a road trip for the same reason you decide to make a change: you want to, you need to, or both. It's a lot of hard work. But remember, like a road trip, a goal trip is supposed to be fun. And reaching the destination will be well worth it.

When you enjoy your trip:

- The time in your car will whoosh by. *Watch out for speeding tickets.*

- You will discover treasures in transit that you would not have seen otherwise.

- It will feel like play, not work.

- Others will notice and want to be part of your journey.

- You will be happy.

Speed Up for a Road Rally

Want some company on your goal trip? There are several official—and a few unofficial—*event* months throughout the year that are designed to encourage people to achieve very specific goals...together.

NaNoWriMo and Camp NaNoWriMo

National Novel Writing Month (NaNoWriMo.org) takes place every November, and I am pretty sure it is the inspiration for all the other months. The challenge is simple. Write a 50,000-word novel in thirty days. Create an account, log into the site, create your profile, and write a novel. Throughout the month, you can upload your word counts to watch your progress as well as get plenty of inspiration, resources, and encouragement. They even have live events in some cities.

Camp NaNoWriMo (CampNaNoWriMo.org) has sessions in April and July and is more like a virtual writers' retreat. The best part about Camp NaNoWriMo is its flexibility. You can choose the project and the word count, up to a million words. Although they suggest new novel drafts, revisions, poetry, scripts, and short stories as project types, I have used both NaNoWriMo and the Camp to work on non-fiction, too.

If you have a burst of time, especially in those two spring and summer months, why not crank out a full draft of your novel, non-fiction book, or articles? You can even write up and store blog posts for the next year. Or use the time to create content for a new course or website.

NaNoEdMo

March is National Novel Editing Month (NaNoEdMo.com). Calendared for three months after NaNoWriMo to give you an ample break, NaNoEdMo's challenge is to log fifty editing hours in one month. This community also has articles on editing, forums for community, and some local events as well as a place to log your time. The trick is that you need to log your editing hours at least once a week and not just the last week of the month.

Again, this is designed for working on a novel, and most of the advice will be specific to that, but you can use the logging tools and encouragement to edit anything.

NaNoPodMo

Also in November is National Podcast Post Month (NaPodPoMo.org). Created by Jennifer Navarrete in 2007, this challenge is to post thirty podcasts in thirty days. It's perfect for jumpstarting or revitalizing a podcast. Your podcast can be audio, video, or both, and the production can range from scrappy (smartphone) to full-on studio quality.

If you want to get into the mode of podcasting regularly and be in a supportive environment, NaNoPodMo is worth a shot.

Plus: NaNoPodMo has a Facebook group for encouragement, support, and posting. Some other awesome podcast pages with related groups include Podcast Movement and She Podcasts.

For more on video, check out VidSummit's page and group and the Mari Smith & Wave Video Challenge Facebook Group. Note: Mari Smith offers lots of insight on Facebook and social media marketing on her regular Facebook page. Also, Dotto Tech has amazing resources for webinars and most things tech.

Other Special Months

Not sure how many poets are reading this, but April is National Poetry Month. Their challenge for NaPoWriMo (NaPoWriMo. net) is to write a poem a day. Nice reason for a creative shake-up in April, don't you think?

National Blog Post Month, formerly a project of BlogHer, encourages bloggers to post every day in November with the hashtag #NaNoBloMo. It's a great way to get into the blogging—or writing—habit. I've seen this hashtag on and off year-round, so you can claim any month as a blog posting month. This brings me to my next point:

If at any point in your journey, you have or can make the time for a monthly challenge, just do it. You can unofficially do any of the already established challenges whenever you want during the year.

Or create a challenge specific to helping you achieve your professional or professional goals. Do thirty instances of anything and track your progress.

For instance:

- Résumé Sending Month

- Find an Investor Month

- Create a Course Month

- Record My Music Month

- Promote Yourself Month

- Get Speaking Gigs Month

- Find a Hobby Month

- Start My Business Month

- Finish Started Projects Month

- Take Care of Me Month

Go over to the *Your Goal Guide* community on Facebook or tweet with the #YourGoalGuide hashtag and let us know what you are doing. We'll support you any time of year.

Slow Down and Enjoy

As you travel from town to town, get out of the car once in a while. Take a nature walk, go on a bike trip, or hike up a literal mountain. Ride the roller coaster at a local fair, see a Broadway show, or dip your toes in the ocean. This is your adventure.

It's not just the destination that's important. Enjoy the ride. You will have many trips in your lifetime: road trips *and* goal trips. And each one will have its own purpose, pluses, and personality.

CONCLUSION
Final Thoughts

I firmly believe that everyone deserves happiness in at least part—if not all—of their lives. If you love your chosen career, that's wonderful. If you have a great personal life, terrific. If your side hustle keeps you excited and energized, fantastic. However, if you are zero for three, you can do one of two things: be okay with being miserable or do something about it.

For those at a crossroads who've decided to make a change, good for you! But don't stop there. That decision is a huge first step. But you need to do the work and follow through. Nearly anything is possible. You just need to take the time to figure out what you want and commit to making it happen.

While you are in charge of your own destiny, as you go through this process, things will happen—personally and professionally. You will have no control over some of these things, and that's okay. If too much "life" gets in the way, step back, take a breath, and give yourself a break. Then, dust yourself off and get back to it.

In the year that led up to my getting the go-ahead to write this book, I lost my primary editing client (position eliminated), and, rather than look for a new job, I made the decision to focus on my mission and rebrand as me. I found an agent (actually, he found me), wrote a book proposal, and got some new clients. Concurrently, I spent more than six months looking for a place to live (they were tearing down my apartment and I had to move) and had to dealt with health issues (mine and others; we're fine), landlords, movers, and other stressors. I try to live without stress, and it was all around me. Yet, I got through it and everything got done.

It's amazing what happens when you chart a course and stick to it. Sometimes it takes longer. Sometimes you have more detours. But you will eventually get there.

APPENDIX A

Worksheets

Road Trip Exercise 1A: GoalTopia

What is your ultimate dream, goal, or accomplishment?

GoalTopia 1:_____

GoalTopia 2:_____

GoalTopia 3:_____

GoalTopia 4:_____

GoalTopia 5:_____

GoalTopia 6:_____

GoalTopia 7:_____

Look at your ideas. Choose one or combine them.

Ultimate GoalTopia:_____

_____

_____

_____

_____

_____

_____

_____

_____

_____

_____

Road Trip Exercise 1B: Visual Representation

Road Trip Exercises 2A and 2B: Current Biography

Highlights

Fill in the following

Employment History:

_____

_____

_____

_____

_____

Education, Organizations, and Certifications:

_____

_____

_____

_____

_____

Successes and Awards:

_____

_____

_____

_____

Strengths (Personal and Professional):

_____

_____

_____

_____

_____

How You Prevailed Over a Challenge:

_____

_____

_____

_____

_____

Skills:

_____

_____

_____

_____

_____

Personal Details and Anecdotes:

_____

_____

_____

_____

_____

Current Biography

Take your information and turn the high points into a bio written in the third person.

_____

_____

_____

_____

_____

_____

_____

_____

_____

_____

Road Trip Exercises 3A and 3B: Future Biography

Highlights

Fill in the following

Future Jobs/Positions/Pursuits:

_____

_____

_____

_____

_____

Education, Organizations, and Certifications:

_____

_____

_____

_____

_____

Dream Awards and Accomplishments:

_____

_____

_____

_____

_____

Future Skills and Talents:

_____

_____

_____

_____

_____

Personal Ambitions:

_____

_____

_____

_____

_____

Future Bios

Take your information and turn the high points into
aspirational bios written in the present tense in the
third person.

One-Year Bio:

_____

_____

_____

_____

_____

_____

_____

_____

Five-Year Bio:

_____

_____

_____

_____

_____

_____

_____

_____

Ten-Year Bio:

_____

_____

_____

_____

_____

_____

_____

Road Trip Exercise 4: Mission Statement

Who are you? What is your background?

_____

_____

_____

What are your values?

_____

_____

_____

What are your unique qualities?

_____

_____

_____

What is your ultimate goal?

_____

_____

_____

What is its value to others?

_____

_____

_____

Put this information together to create your mission statement or fill in the blanks:

Professional: I am a _____ person who enjoys _____ and excels at _____

_____

who wants to help _____

do _____

because _____

_____.

Personal: I am a _____ person who does_____

_____, enjoys _____, and wants to do

_____

in order to _____.

Mission Statement

_____

_____

_____

_____

_____

_____

_____

_____

Road Trip Exercise 5: Motto

Pull five or six keywords that describe the objective from your mission statement.

Keywords:_____

_____

Craft ten potential mottos with those keywords in mind.

Motto 1:_____

Motto 2:_____

Motto 3:_____

Motto 4:_____

Motto 5:_____

Motto 6:_____

Motto 7:_____

Motto 8:_____

Motto 9:_____

Motto 10:_____

Put asterisks next to your three favorites. Then, take a break.

Come back to this worksheet later. Is one of the three the clear winner? Or do you need to add more?

Your Motto

_____

Road Trip Section 1 Review

GoalTopia:

_____

_____

_____

Current Biography:

_____

_____

_____

Future Biography:

_____

_____

_____

Mission Statement:

_____

_____

_____

Motto:

_____

Road Trip Exercise 6: Directed Journaling Prompts

What do I want?

- A new job? A new career? A completely different path?
- What should I do? What excites me about making this change?

Do I want to create or grow something?

- What? A business? A product? A service? What product? What service?
- What reasons do I have for creating, promoting, and pursuing this or any project?
- Why am I the ideal person to create it? How will it help others?

Am I looking to become a known expert?

- What will set me apart?
- Writing a book? Starting a blog, video show, or podcast? Becoming a keynote speaker?
- All of the above? What's first?

Do I need to make a life-change?

- What sort of life-change? What might make me happy?
- What are my options? What are the pros and cons of each?

What does work-life balance look like?

- Change in relationship, location, or home?

- More time for family, friends, dating?

- Find a new hobby, have fun, get healthy?

Road Trip Exercise 7: Common Themes

For each day of journaling, write five things that stand out.

Day 1:

_____

_____

_____

Day 2:

_____

_____

_____

Day 3:

_____

_____

_____

Day 4:

_____

_____

_____

Day 5:

_____

_____

Consistent Ideas:

_____

_____

_____

Omissions:

_____

_____

_____

Additional Insights:

_____

_____

_____

Common Theme:

_____

_____

_____

Road Trip Exercise 8: Options

Option 1:_____

Option 2:_____

Option 3:_____

Option 4:_____

Option 5:_____

Option 6:_____

Option 7:_____

Option 8:_____

Option 9:_____

Option 10:_____

Put asterisks next to the top five. These are the ones you will research more extensively.

Option 1:_____

Why does this interest me?

_____

_____

How will it serve my mission and motto?

_____

_____

In what ways would it be a good fit for my personality/theme?

_____

_____

Which of my experiences and skills can I use or transfer?

_____

_____

What additional education, support, and resources will I need?

_____

_____

Option 2:_____

Why does this interest me?

_____

_____

How will it serve my mission and motto?

_____

_____

In what ways would it be a good fit for my personality/theme?

_____

_____

Which of my experiences and skills can I use or transfer?

_____

_____

What additional education, support, and resources will I need?

_____

_____

Option 3:_____

Why does this interest me?

_____

_____

How will it serve my mission and motto?

_____

_____

In what ways would it be a good fit for my personality/theme?

_____

_____

Which of my experiences and skills can I use or transfer?

_____

_____

What additional education, support, and resources will I need?

_____

_____

Option 4:_____

Why does this interest me?

_____

_____

How will it serve my mission and motto?

_____

_____

In what ways would it be a good fit for my personality/theme?

_____

_____

Which of my experiences and skills can I use or transfer?

_____

_____

What additional education, support, and resources will I need?

_____

_____

Option 5:_____

Why does this interest me?

_____

_____

How will it serve my mission and motto?

_____

_____

In what ways would it be a good fit for my personality/theme?

_____

_____

Which of my experiences and skills can I use or transfer?

_____

_____

What additional education, support, and resources will I need?

_____

_____

Road Trip Exercise 9A: Research

Option 1:_____

What education is required?

_____

_____

What resources exist?

_____

_____

Who are the leaders in the field?

_____

_____

What are the pros?

_____

_____

What are the cons?

_____

_____

Do I want to pursue this path?

_____

Option 2:_____

What education is required?

_____

_____

What resources exist?

_____

_____

Who are the leaders in the field?

_____

_____

What are the pros?

_____

_____

What are the cons?

_____

_____

Do I want to pursue this path?

_____

Option 3:_____

What education is required?

_____

_____

What resources exist?

_____

_____

Who are the leaders in the field?

_____

_____

What are the pros?

_____

_____

What are the cons?

_____

_____

Do I want to pursue this path?

_____

Road Trip Exercise 9B: Connections and Connectors

List Connections:

1:_____

2:_____

3:_____

4:_____

5:_____

6:_____

7:_____

8:_____

9:_____

10:_____

11:_____

12:_____

13:_____

14:_____

15:_____

16:_____

17:_____

18:_____

19:_____

20:_____

21:_____

22:_____

23:_____

24:_____

25:_____

List Connectors:

26:_____

27:_____

28:_____

29:_____

30:_____

31:_____

32:_____

33:_____

34:_____

35:_____

36:_____

37:_____

38:_____

39:_____

40:_____

41:_____

42:_____

43:_____

44:_____

45:_____

46:_____

47:_____

48:_____

49:_____

50:_____

Connections:

Name:_____

Email:_____

Phone number:_____

Website or LinkedIn profile:_____

Notes:_____

_____

Name:_____

Email:_____

Phone number:_____

Website or LinkedIn profile:_____

Notes:_____

_____

Name:_____

Email:_____

Phone number:_____

Website or LinkedIn profile:_____

Notes:_____

_____

Connectors:

Name:_____

Email:_____

Phone number:_____

Website or LinkedIn profile:_____

Notes:_____

_____

Name:_____

Email:_____

Phone number:_____

Website or LinkedIn profile:_____

Notes:_____

_____

Name:_____

Email:_____

Phone number:_____

Website or LinkedIn profile:_____

Notes:_____

_____

Road Trip Exercise 10: Destination Decision

Option 1:_____

Option 2:_____

Option 3:_____

Ask yourself:

Does this choice match my original vision?

Is it aligned with my mission and motto?

Does it support my theme?

What adjustments will I need to make to my life?

Do I want to do this?

GoalTopia Destination:

_____

_____

_____

_____

_____

_____

_____

_____

Road Trip Exercise 11: Goals Brainstorm

1:_____

2:_____

3:_____

4:_____

5:_____

6:_____

7:_____

8:_____

9:_____

10:_____

11:_____

12:_____

13:_____

14:_____

15:_____

16:_____

17:_____

18:_____

19:_____

20:_____

21:_____

22:_____

23:_____

24:_____

25:_____

26:_____

27:_____

28:_____

29:_____

30:_____

31:_____

32:_____

33:_____

34:_____

35:_____

36:_____

37:_____

38:_____

39:_____

40:_____

41:_____

42:_____

43:_____

44:_____

45:_____

46:_____

47:_____

48:_____

49:_____

50:_____

51:_____

52:_____

53:_____

54:_____

55:_____

56:_____

57:_____

58:_____

59:_____

60:_____

61:_____

62:_____

63:_____

64:_____

65:_____

66:_____

67:_____

68:_____

69:_____

70:_____

71:_____

72:_____

73:_____

74:_____

75:_____

76:_____

77:_____

78:_____

79:_____

80:_____

81:_____

82:_____

83:_____

84:_____

85:_____

86:_____

87:_____

88:_____

89:_____

90:_____

91:_____

92:_____

93:_____

94:_____

95:_____

96:_____

97:_____

98:_____

99:_____

100:_____

Road Trip Exercise 12: Professional Goal Map

Long-Term Goal:_____

Short-Term Goal:_____

Benchmark:_____

- Task:_____

- Task:_____

- Task:_____

Benchmark:_____

- Task:_____

- Task:_____

- Task:_____

Benchmark:_____

- Task:_____

- Task:_____

- Task:_____

Short-Term Goal:_____

Benchmark:_____

- Task:_____
- Task:_____
- Task:_____

Benchmark:_____

- Task:_____
- Task:_____
- Task:_____

Benchmark:_____

- Task:_____
- Task:_____
- Task:_____

Road Trip Exercise 12: Professional Goal Map

Long-Term Goal:_____

Short-Term Goal:_____

Benchmark:_____

- Task:_____
- Task:_____
- Task:_____

Benchmark:_____

- Task:_____
- Task:_____
- Task:_____

Benchmark:_____

- Task:_____
- Task:_____
- Task:_____

Short-Term Goal:_____

Benchmark:_____

- Task:_____
- Task:_____
- Task:_____

Benchmark:_____

- Task:_____
- Task:_____
- Task:_____

Benchmark:_____

- Task:_____
- Task:_____
- Task:_____

Road Trip Exercise 12: Professional Goal Map

Long-Term Goal:_____

Short-Term Goal:_____

Benchmark:_____

- Task:_____
- Task:_____
- Task:_____

Benchmark:_____

- Task:_____
- Task:_____
- Task:_____

Benchmark:_____

- Task:_____
- Task:_____
- Task:_____

Short-Term Goal:_____

Benchmark:_____

- Task:_____
- Task:_____
- Task:_____

Benchmark:_____

- Task:_____
- Task:_____
- Task:_____

Benchmark:_____

- Task:_____
- Task:_____
- Task:_____

Road Trip Exercise 13A: Project Personal Goals

Long-Term Goal:_____

Short-Term Goal:_____

Benchmark:_____

- Task:_____
- Task:_____
- Task:_____

Benchmark:_____

- Task:_____
- Task:_____
- Task:_____

Benchmark:_____

- Task:_____
- Task:_____
- Task:_____

Short-Term Goal:_____

Benchmark:_____

- Task:_____
- Task:_____
- Task:_____

Benchmark:_____

- Task:_____
- Task:_____
- Task:_____

Benchmark:_____

- Task:_____
- Task:_____
- Task:_____

Road Trip Exercise 13A: Project Personal Goals

Long-Term Goal:_____

Short-Term Goal:_____

Benchmark:_____

- Task:_____
- Task:_____
- Task:_____

Benchmark:_____

- Task:_____
- Task:_____
- Task:_____

Benchmark:_____

- Task:_____
- Task:_____
- Task:_____

Short-Term Goal:_____

Benchmark:_____

- Task:_____
- Task:_____
- Task:_____

Benchmark:_____

- Task:_____
- Task:_____
- Task:_____

Benchmark:_____

- Task:_____
- Task:_____
- Task:_____

Road Trip Exercise 13B: Lifestyle Goals

Healthy Living:

_____

_____

_____

_____

_____

_____

_____

_____

_____

_____

_____

_____

_____

_____

_____

_____

_____

Road Trip Exercise 13B: Lifestyle Goals

Relationships & Family:

_____

_____

_____

_____

_____

_____

_____

_____

_____

_____

_____

_____

_____

_____

_____

_____

_____

Road Trip Exercise 13B: Lifestyle Goals

Activity:

_____

_____

_____

_____

_____

_____

_____

_____

_____

_____

_____

_____

_____

_____

_____

_____

Road Trip Exercise 13B: Lifestyle Goals

Money:

_____

_____

_____

_____

_____

_____

_____

_____

_____

_____

_____

_____

_____

_____

_____

_____

Road Trip Exercise 13B: Lifestyle Goals

Other:

_____

_____

_____

_____

_____

_____

_____

_____

_____

_____

_____

_____

_____

_____

_____

_____

Road Trip Exercise 14: Priorities

Long-Term Professional Goals:

1._____

2._____

3._____

Long-Term Personal Goals:

1._____

2._____

3._____

Short-Term Professional Goals:

1._____

2._____

3._____

Short-Term Personal Goals:

1._____

2._____

3._____

On-Deck Long-Term Goals:

1._____

2._____

3._____

On-Deck Short-Term Goals:

1._____

2._____

3._____

Road Trip Exercise 15: Alpha Project

Long-Term Goal:_____

Short-Term Goal:_____

Benchmark:_____

- Task:_____
- Task:_____
- Task:_____

Benchmark:_____

- Task:_____
- Task:_____
- Task:_____

Benchmark:_____

- Task:_____
- Task:_____
- Task:_____

Short-Term Goal:_____

Benchmark:_____

- Task:_____

- Task:_____

- Task:_____

Benchmark:_____

- Task:_____

- Task:_____

- Task:_____

Benchmark:_____

- Task:_____

- Task:_____

- Task:_____

Road Trip Exercise 15: Beta Project

Long-Term Goal:_____

Short-Term Goal:_____

Benchmark:_____

- Task:_____
- Task:_____
- Task:_____

Benchmark:_____

- Task:_____
- Task:_____
- Task:_____

Benchmark:_____

- Task:_____
- Task:_____
- Task:_____

Short-Term Goal:_____

Benchmark:_____

- Task:_____
- Task:_____
- Task:_____

Benchmark:_____

- Task:_____
- Task:_____
- Task:_____

Benchmark:_____

- Task:_____
- Task:_____
- Task:_____

APPENDIX B

Resources

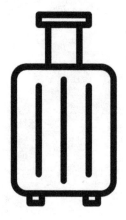

This section has the links mentioned in *Your Goal Guide* as well as additional resources—books, websites, and communities—to help you stay the course, thrive, and achieve your goals.

Connect with Debra

LinkedIn:

- LinkedIn.com/in/Coastbunny

On Facebook:

- *Your Goal Guide* group
- The D*E*B Method page: @TheDEBMethod
- Write On Online page and group: @WriteOnOnline
- Guided Goals Podcast page: @GuidedGoals

On Twitter:

- The D*E*B Method: @TheDEBMethod
- Write On Online: @WriteOnOnline
- GoalChat: @GoalChat

On the Web:

- TheDEBMethod.com
- WriteOnOnline.com
- GuidedGoals.com

Also:

- TheDEBMethod.com/YourGoalGuide
- TheDEBMethod.com/GoalSurvey

- TheDEBMethod.com/GoalChat

Tools

- Meditation Insight Timer: InsightTimer.com
- Graphics: Canva.com
- Mind Map: Mindmapping.com
- Transcribe: Transcribe.wreally.com
- OneNote: OneNote.com
- Evernote: Evernote.com
- Trello: Trello.com

Social Media Platforms

- LinkedIn.com
- Twitter.com
  - Hootsuite: Hootsuite.com
  - TweetDeck: TweetDeck.Twitter.com
  - TweetReports.com for Twitter Chats
  - Follow Madalynsklar.com/2016/09/21/the-very-best-twitter-chats-for-social-media-marketing/
- Facebook.com
- Instagram.com
- YouTube.com

Networking Resources

- Meetup.com
- Eventbrite.com

Special Months

- National Novel Writing Month: NaNoWriMo.org
- Camp NaNoWriMo: CampNaNoWriMo.org
- National Novel Editing Month: NaNoEdMo.com
- National Podcast Post Month: NaPodPoMo.org
- National Poetry Month: NaPoWriMo.net

Support on Facebook:

- NaNoWriMo page and group: @nanowrimo
- NaPodPoMo group
- Podcast Movement page and group: @PodcastMovement
- She Podcasts page and group: @shepodcasts
- Video Makers & Marketers group
- Mari Smith page and group: @marismith
- Dotto Tech page: @DottoTech

Book Recommendations

- *The 4-Hour Workweek* by Timothy Ferriss
- *The 7 Habits of Highly Effective People* by Stephen R. Covey
- *The Artist's Way* by Julia Cameron

- *Eat That Frog!: 21 Great Ways to Stop Procrastinating and Get More Done in Less Time* by Brian Tracy

- *The Frugal Book Promoter* by Carolyn Howard-Johnson

- *Known* by Mark Schaefer

- *The Power of Positive Thinking* by Norman Vincent Peale

- *Rise of the Youpreneur: The Definitive Guide to Becoming the Go-To Leader in Your Industry and Building a Future-Proof Business* by Chris Ducker

- *What Color Is Your Parachute?: A Practical Manual for Job-Hunters and Career-Changers* by Richard N. Bolles

ACKNOWLEDGEMENTS

In order for people to achieve their goals, they must surround themselves with a support system of like-minded individuals. I am beyond blessed to not only be an advocate and cheerleader for others, but to have so many people in my corner.

Thank you to my family, friends, and live and online communities. Thanks to my teachers, mentors, peers, and clients. Thanks to my agent, Paul Levine, and to Chris McKenney, Brenda Knight, and the wonderful team at Mango Publishing. I'm thrilled *Your Goal Guide* landed here with you.

ABOUT THE AUTHOR

A project catalyst and communications specialist, Debra Eckerling, founder of The D*E*B Method, works with individuals and businesses to set goals and manage their projects through one-on-one coaching, workshops, and online support. She speaks on goal-setting, time-management, and productivity, as well as writing, networking, and social media.

Debra has written for national, local, trade, and online publications and has worked in publishing, education, financial services, social media, and technology. Debra received a Bachelor of Arts degree in Journalism from the University of Wisconsin–Madison, where she was an award-winning public speaker on the nationally ranked Forensics team.

She is also the founder of Write On Online, a live and online community for writers, creatives, and entrepreneurs; host of the #GoalChat Twitter Chat and the Guided Goals Podcast; and author of the self-published *Write On Blogging: 51 Tips to Create, Write & Promote Your Blog* and *Purple Pencil Adventures: Writing Prompts for Kids of All Ages.*

Born and raised in the Midwest, Debra now resides in Los Angeles.

Mango Publishing, established in 2014, publishes an eclectic list of books by diverse authors—both new and established voices—on topics ranging from business, personal growth, women's empowerment, LGBTQ studies, health, and spirituality to history, popular culture, time management, decluttering, lifestyle, mental wellness, aging, and sustainable living. We were recently named 2019's #1 fastest growing independent publisher by *Publishers Weekly*. Our success is driven by our main goal, which is to publish high quality books that will entertain readers as well as make a positive difference in their lives.

Our readers are our most important resource; we value your input, suggestions, and ideas. We'd love to hear from you—after all, we are publishing books for you!

Please stay in touch with us and follow us at:

Facebook: Mango Publishing

Twitter: @MangoPublishing

Instagram: @MangoPublishing

LinkedIn: Mango Publishing

Pinterest: Mango Publishing

Sign up for our newsletter at www.mangopublishinggroup.com and receive a free book!

Join us on Mango's journey to reinvent publishing, one book at a time.

CPSIA information can be obtained
at www.ICGtesting.com
Printed in the USA
BVHW081932100220
571928BV00001B/1